JACE'S JOURNEY

DAENNA VAN MULLIGEN

 FriesenPress

One Printers Way
Altona, MB R0G 0B0
Canada

www.friesenpress.com

Copyright © 2022 by Daenna Van Mulligen
First Edition — 2022

All rights reserved.

No part of this publication may be reproduced in any form, or by any means, electronic or mechanical, including photocopying, recording, or any information browsing, storage, or retrieval system, without permission in writing from FriesenPress.

ISBN
978-1-03-915861-0 (Hardcover)
978-1-03-915860-3 (Paperback)
978-1-03-915862-7 (eBook)

1. PETS, DOGS, TRAINING

Distributed to the trade by The Ingram Book Company

To all the dog owners out there who
are struggling—there is hope.

"Do the best you can until you know better.
Then when you know better, do better."
~*Maya Angelou*

This is a true story and reflects the author's undying love for her dog, her diary of his journey, and recollection of events. Some names have been changed to protect the privacy of those depicted.

JACE'S JOURNEY

Preface 1
Forward 2
Introduction 4
Prologue 6
Part 1
Month 1: When You Least Expect It 7
Month 1: OMG We Have a Dog! 12
Month 2: Clueless 15
Part 2
Month 10: Freedom 19
Month 12: Loss & Triumph 23
Month 19: Confusion 25
Month 19: Change of Scenery 29
Part 3
Month 22: Who Knew? 33
Month 23: No Pushing Allowed 37
Part 4
Month 31: Pluses & Minuses 39
Month 31: The Best Laid Plans 43
Month 32: A New Focus 47
Part 5
Month 33: Rock Bottom 49
Month 34: Pharmaceutical Bonanza 53
Month 35: Waiting for a Miracle 55
Month 36: Learning to Trust the Tools 60

Part 6

Month 37: Sniffari 67
Month 38: Need to Evacuate 72
Month 39-43: The Doldrums 75

Part 7

Month 44: Be the Change. 81
Month 45: Not Giving Up. 86
Month 46: Nailed it! 93

Part 8

Month 47: Pepper Spray & First Aid 99
Month 48: Pen to Paper 106
Month 49: Plugging Along. 109
Month 50: Little Things 114

Part 9

Month 51: Bitchy Dog Mom 119
Month 52: Sinking or Swimming 122

Part 10

Month 52: Evolution. 127
Month 53: Saudade. 131
Month 54: When Pigs Fly. 139

Part 11

Month 55: Family Vacation 149
Month 55: My Perfectly Imperfect Boy. 157

Part 12

Be Your Best 161

PREFACE

HI, I'M DAENNA (*DAY-NA*)—STRANGE spelling, simple name.

I assumed I would write a book one day but never considered it would be about a dog, specifically about training a dog.

I assumed it would be a fictional novel, or a book about wine, because that's my job. I'm a wine journalist and have been for nearly two decades.

However, when work slowed down in March of 2020, so did all my usual trips to vineyards around the world. Suddenly I had a lot of time on my hands and a dog that needed profound support.

This is a story of our journey, so far.

I am not a dog trainer and this is not a dog-training book.

I am a human who knows her dog better than anyone else, and has had to step up and put in the hours to make his life more liveable.

So when my husband suggested I write a book about our pilgrimage, I considered it. I had a diary I'd been keeping on his progress, and so many folks had reached out to me for a guidance in the past year, I figured, why not?

FORWARD

I FIRST MET DAENNA on Instagram during my transition to becoming a more open-minded dog behaviourist. I originally started out as someone most people would consider a to be a 'positive only', accredited trainer, which quickly changed after deciding to use an e-collar with my own Romanian rescue dog. I felt honoured for being able to read the first drafts of this book and be a small part of it, as I felt this could help many owners struggling to navigate the confusing world of training a reactive dog.

Reading through the chapters, I felt I finally found someone who was able to articulate the everyday struggles that come with dog behaviour issues. My experience as a reactive dog owner and a professional dog behaviourist was unnervingly similar; from the tension reactive dogs can cause in human relationships to finding the right flow in training, this is exactly what myself and many of my clients had and have been experiencing, during behaviour rehabilitation.

The online dog owner and dog trainer community needs more stories like Jace's. I'm a firm believer that there is no one-size-fits-all training and we need to open the conversation about mixing training methods together, listening to our own instincts and training the dog in front of us. Daenna's bravery might have just done that —being brutally honest about her own feelings, mistakes and challenges as well as being open to try tools that are so frowned upon by people who hardly know anything about them.

The teamwork between Daenna, Barry, Jace and Xoco is truly inspiring. Not only that but the story provides deep insight into living with dogs that exhibit challenging behaviours and how other — often oblivious —dog owners can make life dreadful for both reactive dogs and their guardians. This book is the much needed conversation starter that every dog owner needs to read at least once, whether they have a reactive dog or not.

— Brigitta Orosz Dog Behaviourist,
Owner of Poochology UK
@diaryofareactivedog

INTRODUCTION

THE NUMBER OF NEW dog owners increased dramatically during the global pandemic. Nearly three in 10 Canadians adopted a pet during that time, and of those, nearly 50 percent came from adoption agencies.

Many have behavioural issues; but challenging dogs are not only rescues, many are purebreds created from poor breeding.

But this is not a book about breeding dogs, nor it is a dog-training book.

It is the story of my struggle to help guide a dog with deep-seated foundational fears through life, by learning to cope in an urban environment.

It is a month-by-month snapshot of his life with us so far.

It's a diary of his rehabilitation and my own shortcomings, how I changed my mindset about what a dog truly needs from its human companion while struggling with society's interpretation of my methods.

Over the last few years I've been sharing my struggles and breakthroughs with Jace on social media and discovered I was not alone. So many others are lost or overwhelmed and have reached out for guidance.

Jace's Journey is my way of sharing his story. And just maybe you have one of these troubled dogs in your home and this book will give you the hope and confidence you deserve, to forge your own path with your very unique dog.

If I can do this, so can you.

PROLOGUE

"THERE'S NOTHING MORE I can do for you."

I stared back into the face of my dog trainer—a lovely person—both inside and out; she was kind, encouraging, and exceedingly good at making me feel validated.

My exact response to her when writing this book eluded me, but I do know I felt oddly relieved, and equally heartbroken.

Relieved that it wasn't just me failing my dog, and heartbroken because I had zero idea what was next.

What I didn't realize in that moment was it was best thing that could have happened to us.

In the following weeks, it forced me to take action, to dig in and begin climbing out of a very deep hole.

We had officially hit rock bottom, my dog and me.

PART 1

Month 1: When You Least Expect It

ON A SNOWY SATURDAY on the second weekend of November, I was in Whistler, British Columbia at a ski resort north of Vancouver on Canada's West Coast. As I had done for a decade, I was there to speak at a food and wine festival held annually in the village.

While there I received a message from a friend via social media.

An image of a strange looking dog from a local rescue site was linked to the message. He was far from cute. He was bony and banged up—he was also hairless.

The friend thought of my husband Barry and me, and our hairless duo of cats as soon as she saw him.

She knew Barry had some severe allergies to fur, which is why we had owned the Sphynx breed for nearly 20 years.

Barry and I had always admired certain dogs, I guess we're all innately drawn to a certain breed or physique, and he and I would postulate on what kind of dog we would get if we could. That dog would almost certainly be medium, or on the smaller size of large, with pricked ears and a svelte shape with very short fur.

But it was more a game we would play because we never really thought we'd own one.

Even so we continued year after year to donate generously to the local SPCA.

I had grown up with larger dogs; a Golden Retriever and an Irish Setter. Before those we'd had a couple of elderly Poodles my dad brought into the family when he and my mother married. Barry had also grown up with Poodles. Neither of us had much to do with their care nor feeding.

This dog, a gaunt and awkwardly goofy-looking dog had no coat, save some sparse short*ish* hairs on the top of his head and between his toes.

I read he was a purebred Xoloitzcuintli, and his name was Jason—a ridiculous name for a dog I'd thought.

I had no idea what a Xoloitzcuintli was or how the hell to pronounce the breed name.

Still, I forwarded the image and a note to my husband who was back at home in Vancouver watching over our cats, Seraphina and Petra.

My text to him was something along the lines of, "Looking for a home!"

He didn't get the gist of the message; he just thought I'd sent him the image of some malnourished random dog and responded with a vague, "Poor guy."

I translated his comment as a complete lack of interest.

I left it at that because I was the traveller in the family.

Work would take me away for a couple months scattered throughout of the year and the care and feeding of the crew was all up to him on those occasions. Not to mention our youngest cat Petra had always been sickly; she needed extra attention, and daily meds.

The next night, Sunday, I was home and all four of us were cuddled up on the sofa—the humans drinking wine, the cats soaking up our body heat.

For some reason I brought up Jason.

It was then Barry realized I wanted us to consider adopting him.

He was hairless—we never knew there was a natural breed of hairless dogs—and he needed a home. Pulling up his photo again was like fate giving us a swift kick in the ass. His eyes were the clincher; they were incredibly soulful and spoke to us on a deep level. In a quick verdict, we decided to apply to foster-to-adopt Jason—I sent the paperwork in on Monday morning.

On Tuesday, Furever Freed Rescue contacted us to organize a home visit on Thursday, November 16th. We were told we weren't first in queue for him, which made us anxious; we were attached already, and not getting Jason would have been a huge blow.

The site visit went extremely well and we felt confident, but until we were certain we tried not to get our hopes too high.

Friday the 17th, just after noon, I received a phone call that our foster-to-adopt had been accepted.

Jason would be arriving by air from Cabo San Lucas, Mexico, on November 25th.

We started researching the breed, collecting as much information on their traits and instincts as we could: skittish, highly intelligent, very agile, high prey drive and Velcro to their person but aloof with other humans; that was only the tip of the Xolo iceberg.

They had webbed paws, a percentage was born coated—thanks to a recessive gene—and the hairless versions not only lacked fur, but complete dentition.

Xolos, like the Peruvian Inca Orchid and Chinese Crested breeds, carry a hairless gene called FOXI3. What they lack in fur they make up for in keratin, so their nails grow extremely fast, but it also meant they were prone to blackheads made up of keratic substances.

We practiced pronouncing Xoloitzcuintli (*show-low-eat-squeent-lee*) and stocked up on all the items we thought Jason would need while impatiently waiting for November 25th to arrive.

JACE'S JOURNEY

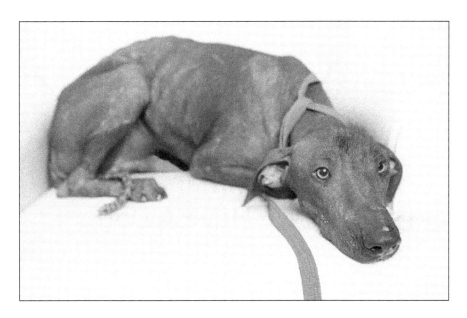

*Jace (formerly Jason) at the Casa Sheila Rescue in
Cabo San Lucas, Mexico. Photo: Casa Sheila*

*Jace (formerly Jason) at the Casa Sheila Shelter in
Cabo San Lucas, Mexico. Photo: Casa Sheila*

Month 1: OMG We Have A Dog!

BARRY AND I WERE waiting in the arrivals area of Vancouver International Airport late on that chilly November night.

In our car's backseat a massive blanket awaited to keep our hairless Jason warm.

Then a luggage cart stacked with dog crates rolled toward us; we could barely make out Jason in the largest bottom crate.

He was curled up looking curious but also anxious; when I reached out with my hand toward the crate he came right to me.

He was so beautiful.

His time at the Casa Sheila shelter in Mexico had been good to him, he'd filled out a bit, and roaming the shelter's yard in the sunshine had turned his skin from an ashy grey to black-mahogany.

After some photos, paperwork and necessary housekeeping tips from Furever Freed we were ready to go.

Our new 10-to-11 month old pup jumped into our car with zero hesitation when prompted. He must have been in shock, arriving in winter to a cold and wet Vancouver. Luckily we had bought him warm clothing in advance.

Jason—whom we decided to call Jace—was home and almost immediately had an Instagram account: *@showmethexolo*.

Upon arrival, our greatest fear was introducing Jace to our cats; we knew the breed had high prey drive, so the introduction had to be done with the utmost time and care.

However, as soon as we walked in the house with Jace on leash, our senior cat Seraphina trotted right down the stairs until she was eye level with him. She stretched her neck out to sniff at him.

His nose touched hers and that was it.

Neither of our cats had ever encountered a dog, so they had zero fear.

If anything, to this day, I'd say Jace was more fearful of them.

We really had a dog.

Over the next week or so, we would take short walks with Jace for potty breaks. We noticed his hesitancy and skittishness around everything outside but chalked it up to being a new rescue in a new city.

Then one day while running errands, we decided to take him with us.

Those errands needed to be done in one of the busiest areas around our neighbourhood where two major city intersections crossed, and there was a cacophony of vehicular noise, foot traffic and shops.

At first Jace seemed okay, his usual shy self. We took him into the local pet store and into our insurance agency to renew our car insurance; he was curious and friendly, almost eager to say hi to people in those places.

Then we approached a major intersection and it was like a switch went off. He had a full-blown panic attack. He began pulling Barry along like a dog twice the size of his slender 20-kilo (44 pound) frame.

Looking back I'm surprised (and mortified at the thought) the narrow fabric collar we had him on didn't break.

There were too many triggers, he was overwhelmed and something finally snapped.

From that point onward, it seemed like everything was even more frightening to him. Cars, bikes, strollers, loud noises, and even people just walking past or behind us would cause his tail to wrap under his belly and his head to swivel constantly looking for danger. He never wanted to leave the house, and when he did it was for a quick pee and that was it.

He started to react explosively to other dogs in his vicinity.

I tried a well-known fitted canine calming shirt, but he would collapse to the floor when anything touched his back; ergo the tight shirt was a complete disaster. I tried calming sprays, aromatics and collars. They did nothing.

We would walk him in the very early mornings and at night when the streets were quiet. I didn't know anything; I didn't know if this was typical of a new rescue, and if I could train it out of him.

I was clueless.

Month 2: Clueless

WE KNEW IMMEDIATELY WE'D wanted to officially adopt Jace, so we cut short the foster portion of the contract with Furever Freed and moved right on to making it official. On December 5th we drove out to the rescue's vet near Langley. My parents, who lived in Abbotsford, drove to meet us, and their first grand-puppy.

Jace showed notable reticence leaving our sides or the safety of our car. He was almost feral as we tried to lure him from the vehicle to the vet's office—attempting to drag us back to the car. Once inside he was calmer. His reaction to meeting people was aloof curiosity but he remained vigilant and skittish. The vet checked him over, micro-chipped him, and we signed the paperwork making him completely ours.

Naively we held out hope his fear was the result of him being a new rescue.

As the month progressed, we knew it was more than that.

So on December 30th a local trainer recommended to us made a home visit.

The trainer was extremely pragmatic, almost robotic. She observed Jace in our house and watched me walking him outside.

Her conclusion, "He's terrified."

I already knew that. Jace was afraid of the world. The only place he was at ease was in the confines of our home. Period.

The trainer recommended a better diet and a couple of complex dog books to purchase.

I didn't warm up to her, and I personally didn't feel like we had any more direction than before. I concluded this was the dog I had; I would work around his fears.

Solid pointers on using a treat bag and high quality treats, as well as a clicker, was what I did get from that consultation—she also directed me on transitioning Jace to a raw diet, which I'm grateful for.

Following her visit I began my own research online, implemented the clicker and bought a martingale collar. I wasn't entirely confident with what I was doing with the clicker, but it still worked for the most part.

I used it to distract Jace from looking at other dogs; when I clicked, he looked at me, and when he looked at me he got a treat.

It worked 90-percent of the time, just not when we were in close proximity to another dog. Then all the cheese in the world wouldn't stop him from going berserk. His explosions always occurred in a nanosecond and I could never quite catch or prevent the moment they would happen.

JACE'S JOURNEY

Jace and Petra

PART 2
Month 10: Freedom

THE PREVIOUS EIGHT MONTHS of life had become routine. Jace slept in his crate in our bedroom and remained in it whenever we left the house.

We had lost our eldest cat Seraphina in March due to complications from surgery. She was 13 years old and her death had hit us hard.

Petra was melancholic and relied even more on us for comfort. She even warmed up to Jace and would often curl up with him, much to his dismay.

It almost seemed like he was afraid he'd hurt her.

Petra's epilepsy had been getting progressively worse in recent years. She'd had brain surgery, constant respiratory infections, several MRIs, and a vet file two inches thick—she needed a lot of care.

We focused on her.

I knew little more about Jace's issues; he was still highly fearful, was still reactive to other dogs, and would even bark at random people as if to tell them to back away. He still preferred to be inside and would only poop in one spot in the very early morning before people were out and commuter traffic began.

I could get him to walk no more than 30 meters from our home, usually less. If he got startled before he peed, we'd have to retreat to our front door and repeat the whole process. If he decided he wasn't going to go in a direction, we didn't go. He would shut down; literally freeze, plant his paws, get low, and start backing up—toward home.

I wore a heavy-duty hip belt when I walked him; I didn't trust he wouldn't drag me down if he reacted to another dog. Jace wasn't quite done growing, but even at his current weight of 25 kilo (55 pounds), he was amazingly strong.

On the weekends Barry and I would get up as the sun rose and take him for a longer walk together. We were able to weave down lanes and quieter streets to the False Creek Seawall where, if lucky, we wouldn't pass any other dogs.

That was the extent of Jace's exercise—two longer weekend morning walks.

We'd come to terms with his challenges because that's all we knew to do.

Around 6:30 a.m., on August 4th of the B.C. Day long-weekend, we walked by a local off-leash dog park called Charleson Park. Located along False Creek, Charleson is only one of Vancouver's beautiful off-leash seaside parks.

A bouncy young black doodle named Ron came running toward us, stopping at the fence between the park and the seawall. Jace did his usual reactive, lunge, growl, and bark-dance routine. Ron's owner sauntered up to the fence and we started talking. After a few minutes Jace stopped being reactive and was suddenly chill. He simply ignored Ron.

That was a first.

Ron's owner suggested we bring Jace into the park and let them play.

Barry and I looked at each other, both thinking, "No way."

But Jace was being so calm, and Ron's owner was convincing; we made a snap decision to take him into the park and drop the leash. It was one of the most unforgettable moments of my life. Jace ran and played, he was gleeful to be able to just run; and run he did. He was fast, so fast, and so suddenly confident.

I might have cried a little—for the first time in the nine months we'd had him, he was utterly free.

The park became a routine—weekend mornings specifically, because it was the quietest time of the day. There were fewer dogs and the people and dogs that did come to the park at that time of day became our friends. We trusted them and their dogs. Ron became Jace's bestie and they played extremely well together.

For the most part we had no issues off-leash. A couple small spats arose from dogs who started getting chippy with Jace when they couldn't catch him, but nothing too concerning.

Barry and I were always very watchful—almost hovering, especially when new dogs came into the park. Jace's speed made dogs want to chase him, and the park was not fully enclosed.

If we were together, Barry would likely chat with other dog owners and I would stand a good distance away. I always wanted

Jace to be able to escape the fray of humans and canines if he needed; I wanted to be his safety.

If I was alone I didn't converse much with others, my attention never left Jace. If I didn't like a dog or a situation, I exited the park.

Jace at Charlson Park Dog Park Photo: Barry Komar

Month 12:
Loss & Triumph

IN OCTOBER WE SAID good-bye to our baby girl Petra.

The night of October 24th, she went into a cluster of seizures that just couldn't be stopped. I cut short a wine trip I'd been on in the Okanagan Valley, flying home on the morning of the 25th—I held her, weeping, as she took her last breath that very night.

Jace could feel our heartbreak—I don't think he personally mourned her loss, rather he felt our grief.

After nearly two decades as a cat-only family, within less than one year we became a dog-only family.

With Petra's passing came a realization of how exhausting it had been in the last few years caring for her. Just leaving the house had been stressful, never knowing if she could have an episode while we were away.

With her loss came a twisted sort of freedom.

We began taking Jace to the park weekdays in the afternoons as well as weekends. We saw this as a huge win. Once he realized the scary daytime walks resulted in off-leash time and playing with other dogs, he was much more accepting. Sure, he was still highly anxious of all noises—people, cars, bikes and almost anything else on the walk there, and we avoided other on-leash dogs, except his known friends.

There was a moment that really stuck with me on one of those days.

We were walking down the quiet 7th avenue on our way home from the park when we tried to pass another dog. I had hoped Jace would keep his cool, he tended to be more placid post off-leash sessions, but we were too close, mere meters away. Jace erupted, spitting, lunging and growling, and we froze.

All hell broke loose—I was glued to the spot just holding Jace back, and the other dog began to react in turn.

Finally the other dog's owner yelled at me to, "Just move on!"

I walked away thinking, wow, what a nasty woman.

It took me a couple more years to understand why she was so angry and how obtuse I had been.

Month 19: Confusion

OVER THE NEXT EIGHT months the dog park continued to be an integral part of our social life. Not only for Jace, but also for Barry, myself, and the new owner friends we had made.

Then one morning in May something changed.

All three of us were in the park with the usual crew.

An off-leash puppy came bounding down the path into the park. A woman running after the golden pup started yelling in a high-pitched and stressed voice for her pup to come back to her, which of course, it did not.

I watched it all unfold in slow motion. I thought, why was her pup off-leash—the pathways into the park were not dedicated as off-leash—and running ahead of her, and why was she so upset?

Her puppy ran into the park and everyone stopped talking because the woman sounded like she was in a full-blown panic. As she ran into the park after her pup, I shouted to her, "Flight risk?" She pointed and said, "No, that dog attacked my dog before."

She was pointing at Jace.

Taken aback, I said, "No he hasn't, that's my dog and I've never seen you or your dog before."

At this point she had reached her puppy and was on her knees holding it.

I had a very bad feeling.

Someone suggested it might have been another dog that looked like Jace.

Everyone in the park at that moment knew Jace and had never seen him so much as growl at another dog in the park. Knowing that was highly unlikely, that I only knew of one other standard Xolo in the city, I said, "No there are no other dogs like Jace."

I ignored the woman and my instinct to leave.

Barry was quiet the whole time, but I could sense his discomfort.

I suppose I stayed out of vanity, I wanted her to see that Jace was not a dog that attacked other dogs. But within five minutes something happened.

Jace did go after her puppy. To this day we have no idea why.

He did not hurt the pup, he ran at it in an aggressive manner, scared the hell out of it, and the puppy started squealing and toppled onto its side.

We left the park immediately after that incident.

We were horrified and bewildered.

Barry told me later he was with Jace in the park a week or so prior. He forgot Jace did something similar to a small dog, but nothing happened and he blew it off. Thinking back, he realized it was likely the same puppy.

We were suddenly concerned and extra careful. We avoided the park if we saw her and her dog.

Then it happened again.

We were in the park with Jace; he was playing with other dogs as usual. The same puppy, again off-leash, came running into the park, the owner so far behind it we couldn't even see her.

Immediately a switch in Jace flipped and he went after it. Again, he did not hurt the dog, but this time we knew something had changed.

We were so angry—angry that this woman didn't follow the law and leash her dog until they arrived at the park. She never did. If she had, we could have at least had the opportunity to leash Jace and leave. Instead she continued to insist on letting her puppy run ahead of her into possible danger.

In the end we'd be to blame if Jace ever hurt her dog.

Believe it or not, years later, I still see the same woman with that fully grown dog off leash, all the time.

Barry and I were extremely resentful.

We lost our local hang out, Jace's freedom, and friends we had made.

The author, walking with Jace on the seawall. Photo: Barry Komar

Month 19: Change of Scenery

AFTER REALIZING OUR GLORY days at nearby Charleson Park were gone, we had to find a new place for Jace to play.

We decided on Spanish Banks' off-leash dog area because if there was one thing we were strict on, off-leash play was only done in off-leash areas.

The region was several acres in size with a nice grassy area alongside the beach—and it wasn't terribly busy in the mornings. As a bonus we could take Jace out onto the tidal flats at low tide. There were literally kilometres of space to run when the tides were low enough.

The first four or five times we put Jace in the car to take him to the beach he peed in the car. He panted, whined, paced, circled, and shook his body hard, flapping his ears aggressively. The shaking and flapping we were used to. It was his coping mechanism. He shook off stress to reset himself. With his high level of anxiety at all times you can imagine how often he needed to reset.

That same year we'd discovered his ear tips starting to crack and bleed because he shook so fiercely. It became chronic; mostly occurring in the colder months but there was never a seasonal guarantee. Lotion and snoods helped, but once an ear tip was open our house turned into a crime scene—blood everywhere.

We'd tried sticky bandages of all sorts, tape, liquid bandages, you name it; nothing truly worked.

To this day it's an issue.

Once we'd arrive at Spanish Banks, Jace would calm down somewhat. But until he was off-leash and playing for a while, he remained tightly strung. We didn't realize all that pent up anxiety building in the car was often translating to irrational behaviour off-leash.

Jace revelled in his off-leash time though. Besides being at home, off-leash in open spaces was his happy place. He remained good at sticking close to us, so we were comfortable with his freedom overall, but his recall was only good when he wanted it to be good. If there were any things more interesting than us—such as another dog—he'd totally blow us off.

We found a few early morning weekend regulars on our visits, and Jace played well with all those dogs.

In mid-May we stumbled upon our dream home one Sunday during an open house. It was nearby our current residence, but directly on the False Creek waterfront, settled on a quiet private laneway. It needed a lot of work, but we had the time.

A huge deciding factor in that move was how peaceful the neighbourhood was.

In our current home there was a teardown and looming construction of a new condominium complex about to commence—directly across the street. Right behind us a new high-rise was slated go up in the next couple of years.

We knew all that would be horrible for Jace; we weren't looking for more anxiety.

So we bought the townhouse confident we would all be far happier there.

Low tide at Spanish Banks in the off-leash area

PART 3
Month 22: Who Knew?

AFTER TAKING POSSESSION OF our new home at the beginning of July we went into full-on renovations. Through the course of construction we were sure to bring Jace over on the weekends when the contractor wasn't around. We wanted him to get to know the place, so that when we finally made the move he would have some semblance of comfort.

He peed all over the house. Downstairs, on the stairs, upstairs… Luckily it was all being replaced.

On August 13th, two weeks before move in, I had a consultation with a highly recommended local trainer. I'll admit I immediately adored her. Her vibrancy and positivity were contagious, and her knowledge impressive. She didn't make me feel like a failed owner—she was highly observant, and supportive.

She knew we were relocating soon and needed help acclimating Jace.

That first session we worked primarily on confidence building; getting Jace to step on items like boxes and stools, and getting him to put his nose into buckets for treats; things I had never considered.

Indoors we started working on tricks like *spin* and *shake-a-paw*—outdoors jumping up on things such as logs, benches, and rocks.

Jace loved the engagement with me, and like the stacks of puzzle toys we'd bought for him, he picked things up quickly.

The trainer could see how skittish he was indoors; she immediately called our vet suggesting he be put on sedatives to calm his nerves. We didn't know prescription meds were a possibility, but if they helped relieve some of Jace's stress, we were all for it.

On August 19th we started him on a daily dose of Fluoxetine. Also known as Prozac, Fluoxetine was commonly prescribed anti-depressant used for the treatment of major depressive disorders and obsessive–compulsive disorder (OCD). We were warned it would take six-to-eight weeks to see any improvement.

While the move on August 26th went smoothly, there were suddenly challenges with Jace we never expected. Our quiet tree-lined lane did just the opposite of what we thought; it threw Jace into a tailspin of dread.

Every rustling leaf, window reflection and small sound made him panic. There were corners everywhere—people and dogs would appear from nowhere, startling him, and he'd going into full-blown panic attacks. If it were a dog, he would react explosively; a person, he'd drag us back to our front gate.

Just getting him to pee took incredible effort—and he would do it in one spot only, on an elevated mound under a tree where he was above the lane and protected on two sides. He abruptly refused to walk in any direction from home. We started bringing the car from the garage around to our front gate just to get him into it for beach times.

He seemed much more fearful now than in our old home, and again, we were at a loss.

On August 30th, days after the move, we had a follow up visit with the trainer.

She was shocked at how paralyzing Jace fears truly were. She had only worked with him in the house and I could see in her eyes the realization of how terrified he was outside. He reminded her of the wolves she used to work with, she told me—constantly surveying and untrusting.

She also noted his barrier reactivity—meaning any dog that walked by when we were in our yard he would react to with extreme aggression and rush the fence. Thankfully he never showed any inclination to jump the gate. He was simply trying to scare other dogs away.

Obviously the dogs complied—at least in his mind—as they were just walking by anyway.

The trainer suggested putting visual barriers up around our fence—which we did—and we worked on more indoor confidence building skills and clicker training.

I understood the clicker concept. As I had been doing previously, she had me clicking whenever Jace looked at anything that might cause him to react, and then treating him when he didn't.

What confused me was waiting for something to trigger a reaction; it set me on edge; having treats within speedy reach at all times was nearly impossible. Being on top of a possible explosion was all consuming when his reactions seemingly came with zero warning.

Nothing about the advice seemed instinctual to me.

After our sessions I always felt shortly buoyed, the trainer gave wonderful pep talks, but by the next day, when reading through her laundry list of *to-dos* everything seemed daunting again, and I deflated. I felt like a hamster on a wheel, I didn't know where I was going, except in circles.

I held out hope Jace's meds would kick in soon.

Spanish Banks off-leash dog area

Month 23:
No Pushing Allowed

OUR NEXT TRAINING SESSION was on September 13th.

Jace had been on Fluoxetine for less than a month, so there was little expectation of change since she had seen him last.

He'd not improved one iota, but the visual barrier around our yard did help his home turf reactivity somewhat. Our new neighbours Don and Nina had a friendly Frenchie named Decker—if Jace could see Decker through the fence he would literally tear his paws bloody trying to get through the fence at him. It was bad enough when Jace heard or smelled Decker, but visual confirmations turned explosive.

Great new neighbours, huh?

Luckily, throughout their marriage Don and Nina had several dogs, and experience with behavioural issues; they got it.

In that training session, among other things, we focused on getting Jace to simply walk down the lane. From our gated yard Jace and I would exit. I would click and throw a piece of cheese ahead a few feet while bending downward and forward at the hips, angling my body toward Jace. As soon as he picked up the cheese I would repeat the process. If he so much as looked up and realized where he was and panicked, I was directed to quickly return home. The trainer didn't want him to stress.

She also had me pay close attention to Jace's body language to determine the moment he was showing signs of a meltdown; at that point we would quickly turn him around toward home. We did this time and time again. Once or twice we got as far as 10 meters down the lane, but overall it was far less.

I could see what our destination looked like, but I couldn't envision the path to get there. It felt monumental, like an overgrown jungle I'd have to hack my way through. It also seemed to require a lot of cheese tossing while my middle-aged body was contorted in an unsustainable position. Not to mention, what would I do in that hunched position if another dog rounded the corner toward us?

I was struggling.

PART 4
Month 31: Pluses & Minuses

SOMETIME IN MARCH WE decided, along with our vet, that the Fluoxetine was not working; why bother having him on medication that just didn't work?

By May we'd weaned him off.

On May 12th our trainer made another visit—the first in eight months, since the previous September. This visit had an entirely different focus.

In one week we were expecting a new puppy!

Puppy would be arriving from Mexico City at 10-weeks old, and as excited as we were, we were uneasy about bringing another dog into the house with such a territorial Jace. Deep down we knew he was a gentle dog, but we weren't taking chances. She was born on March 1—one of six hairless Xolos in a litter of seven. I had been following the breeder on Instagram for a while and when they posted the birth announcement I contacted them immediately.

Earlier in the year, in January, we tried to adopt another standard Xolo named Luis, a rescue from Puerto Vallarta, but the family in queue ahead of us fell in love with him and we missed out. Looking back it was for the best, having another male rescue, one with his own issues and more so, one that might challenge Jace's position, likely would have ended badly.

When I reached out to the pup's breeder in Mexico City, I was first in line and selected the two I preferred of the four females. Little miss purple ribbon and little miss white ribbon.

I didn't tell Barry, per se, I just showed him photos of the cute baby Xolos every so often to soften him up.

Over the following weeks I had the breeder send me images and updates of the two girls playing and engaging with their littermates. I asked which was the most confident and outgoing. Little miss white ribbon was it. Additionally she looked more like her dam, with a smaller pointier nose, which more closely resembled Jace's.

By the time they were about eight weeks old I told Barry I wanted her.

He wasn't on board initially, but I won him over.

To honour her Aztec ancestry, we decided to name her Xoco, pronounced SHŌ-kō (Nahuatl for *little one* or *little sister*), and awaited her arrival with excitement and trepidation.

The May 12th session was also about Jace's leash and barrier aggression.

The trainer recommended we reach out to one of Vancouver's leading vet behaviourists about Jace's fears, and ways to deal with the approaching arrival of Xoco.

That day the trainer also brought her stuffed dog—a middle-to-large sized black prop she used specifically to test reactivity or aggression. In the lane outside our gate, she set it up attached to a leash she held, and had Jace and I emerge.

Jace reacted instantaneously.

She told me to release leash pressure and let him come sniff the prop dog; hesitantly I let him pull me across the lane to the prop. The moment he got to the prop dog, he immediately stopped reacting and sniffed its fake butt.

This was proof she said, that he's not aggressive; he was fear reactive on leash and had barrier frustration.

We did that same test several times and finally Jace ignored the prop entirely.

I was so buoyed by her words I reached out to Nina and asked if she was interested in having Jace meet Decker on neutral ground at Kits Beach, a local off-leash park.

What I did, or didn't do next, still haunts me—I didn't read the room, or in this case Jace.

We took the car to the beach and it was busy; so very busy.

There were dozens of dogs and people milling about. I didn't yet know about thresholds, and he was approaching his quickly. In my ignorance I didn't turn around and take him home. I unwittingly let his anxiety build as we got closer to the shoreline, then let him off his leash.

By the time Nina and Decker arrived, Jace was over threshold and went right after Decker. Luckily he didn't use his teeth, but he rolled Decker under him and stood over him in a power move, spitting and barking.

Decker didn't back down.

Still, I grabbed Jace and pulled him off Decker, leashing him and walking away from the scene as Barry and Nina made sure Decker was okay.

He was.

I was less than fine and Jace did not deserve my stupidity.

After the incident at the beach, I was going over the trainer's recommendations from her May 12th visit and started asking myself how I would feel if I let Jace approach another dog on-leash, not a prop dog, and he didn't act the same way as he did with the prop?

The point was never to put pressure on the leash when around another dog, or it would create frustration, which long term could lead to aggression. But in those situations, Jace was creating his own pressure by pulling toward the triggers. I was bewildered; I didn't trust my own instincts in those situations, and I didn't trust Jace.

At that point, Xoco's arrival was taking precedence, so I pushed everything else aside. We weren't getting any farther down the lane with Jace anyway, and I was stumped on what to do next. I knew that we couldn't work on leash reactivity just stationed outside our gate; we needed to get Jace to actually go for walks and work through those sorts of issues on neutral ground.

Naively perhaps, I believed having a playmate—a confident young female companion, could bring Jace out of his shell, and show him what being a dog was all about.

Month 31: The Best Laid Plans

MUCH TO OUR DISAPPOINTMENT, Xoco's May 16th arrival was delayed a week due to a miscommunication with the airline and customs in Mexico City.

Honestly, I think the extra week with her siblings in a newly antisocial COVID world was for the best.

On the night of May 21st we waited in the cargo area of her airline of transport. Delay after delay, mistake upon mistake—we were beside ourselves. We could hear Xoco crying in her kennel and could do nothing but wait.

Once released, I opened the shipping kennel and she was almost feral as she curled into the back growling at me. Leaving her be, I put her in the car and left the kennel door open allowing her to make a move on her own. By the time we'd driven two blocks she was in Barry's arms in the passenger seat and looking at him like he was her saviour.

I recall saying to him, tears in my eyes, "Oh my God she's more beautiful than the photos, and she's going to be a daddy's girl."

It was late when we arrived home—too late to attempt the projected Jace and Xoco meet on neutral territory. Let's be honest, a dog that didn't walk outside his own home wasn't going to agree to a neutral territory meet-cute anyway.

So I winged it.

I put Xoco in her new extra-large crate in the foyer, closed off from the living room where Jace was freely roaming. When I let him come out and sniff her, he circled the crate looking a bit predatory and rushed it twice sort of growling. This time I could openly see his frustration at not being able to get to her. It wasn't aggression. Still, we knew it could be weeks before they would physically encounter each other.

The best laid plans and all.

After a sleepless night of Xoco whining in her shipping kennel beside our bed, and Jace in his own bed alongside ours, we woke to a reality of two dogs, and twice the work.

It's a bit of a blur, but the very next morning, we were letting Jace sniff Xoco while Barry held her. Then the slippery little miss was out of his arms and the introduction we expected in a week or more happened.

My heart stopped; time stood still. And just like that, they were playing.

I'm not saying there weren't bumps in the coming weeks; he did scare her a few times, was a bit too pushy once or twice, and resource guarded me once—for which he was reprimanded. But she was pure sunshine and joy, and she made Jace happy, like he had something to look forward to each day.

We all got very lucky—she was the perfect addition.

Xoco and the author

Xoco and Jace

Month 32:
A New Focus

IF I KNEW ONE thing, it was this; Xoco needed to have all the opportunities Jace never did. So I threw myself into her training and socialization. Having a confident companion, a dog to show Jace how to be a dog, and a playmate, were primary reasons for getting a second dog. I couldn't fail her—and therefore him— in her early weeks and months. Putting Jace on the backburner wasn't the plan, but I knew I needed to get her on solid footing before I could get back to figuring out how to move forward with Jace.

Our trainer got a puppy just a week or two after Xoco arrived, so that made for easy puppy play-dates. I started taking the trainer's puppy zoom classes each week and learned so much about the basics of training and doling out plenty of high value treats. Topics I was sorely lacking on.

In those first couple months I took Xoco everywhere: to playgrounds and heavy-duty construction sites, and to the busiest intersections in Vancouver. I played controlled sounds of thunder and fireworks to her, worked on recall and leash manners, took her to restaurant patios and into big box, and pet stores. She had playdates with several puppies we met through training classes.

Meanwhile Jace was regressing.

He was starting to get separation anxiety when I left with her and was defecating and peeing all around the downstairs the moments I was out of sight.

While Xoco was potty trained by 16-weeks, he was messing every time I went out.

His nerves got so bad he was outwardly refusing to go outside to pee.

No matter how much cheese, boiled chicken, organic all beef wieners I threw out he wouldn't step more than a meter out the door. We begged, dragged, pleaded, and finally started carrying him to the gate.

I dreaded each time I had to take Jace out. I was exhausted, I was depressed, and I cried—every single day.

Each time I would try and take him out he just wouldn't go. I hated dragging him, I was worried we were hurting him—would do damage to him. I would sit on our stairs and cry. Jace would drop his head and move slowly toward me, nudging me. It was like he was apologizing, but we just weren't connecting—we weren't communicating.

One day I hit my emotional wall. I told Barry Jace was miserable with us and we had to find a new home for him. Somewhere out in the country where he didn't have to worry about people and cars—somewhere he could live a happier life.

Obviously that didn't happen. Barry talked me off that proverbial ledge.

PART 5

Month 33: Rock Bottom

ON JULY 6TH, under guidance of our family vet we decided to put Jace back on Fluoxetine as we waited for our initial consultation with the vet behaviourist.

Earlier that same day I had taken Jace to Spanish Banks. I felt he needed, and deserved, my full attention. He needed to have a good run.

It was low tide, so we had plenty of room to roam with him off-leash.

In the distance, a woman and a large dog were walking at 30-degree angle toward us, so I swung wide as we kept walking. I saw her put her dog on leash just before Jace took off toward them barking his ass off while circling them.

The woman yelled to me as I was trying to recall Jace, that my dog was being very aggressive. I yelled back, "Don't worry, he's not aggressive."

She retorted, that his behaviour was in fact, very aggressive.

I ignored her, recalled Jace and we kept walking in the opposite direction.

I was getting a sick feeling.

On July 7th I had a follow up visit with the trainer. Jace's lack of progression, not even being able to walk down our lane after living there for almost a year was proof his issues were far deeper than she realized. She was unable to help him, to help us.

"There's nothing more I can do for you."

My recollection of my response that day eludes me, but I know I felt oddly relieved, and equally heartbroken. Relieved that it wasn't just me failing my dog, and heartbroken because I had zero idea what was next.

We had officially hit rock bottom, Jace and me, so I was relying on the vet behaviourist to come through.

That consult came two days later, on July 9th.

A truly kind and respected doctor, she spent two hours with us, asking questions about everything from Jace's early life and rescue, to fears and diet. She observed him as we sat outside in our yard, his reaction to every little leaf movement, window reflection, and street noise and how quickly he recovered from a reaction to passing person or dog.

We talked about his sensitivity to any back touch, as well as his sometimes-shitty social skills. She explained to me how trigger stacking worked, and Jace's likely low threshold.

> Each time a dog is exposed to a stressor, or trigger, those triggers—especially when occurring sequentially, stack, causing increased arousal, until the dog reaches its threshold and is no longer able to cope. This often results in unpredictable behaviours such as reacting, or shutting down.

I told her the story of the dog at Spanish Banks just days earlier. It had been weighing on me and I didn't blame the other dog's owner. I would have been angry if a dog had done that to Jace.

Even so, she agreed with the trainer and said it was imperative to continue to socialize him off-leash with other dogs. But she was also clear that if anyone reported Jace, if his behaviour seemed aggressive, he would have a permanent record.

I did not agree about off-leash play, but they were the experts. Barry was feeling equally as reluctant as I was when it came to off-leash socialization.

Our biggest concern: one of those few dogs Jace did get chippy with would not put up with his crap and retaliate. Even with their thick skin, having no fur made Xolos vulnerable, and I knew Jace could be badly injured.

I needed to have a rock solid recall if I was going to continue to let him play with strange dogs.

Not knowing where to go from there, I reached out to a friend I had met through social media. She lived two hours south of me in Washington State and had a Xolo as well. Jess and I had talked about Jace's issues in the past. She had made a few suggestions on how to help him get over some of his most basic fears, but in reality, no one knew how bad things were until they saw Jace in the flesh.

Jess had been hesitant to suggest using balanced training methods on Jace, as she didn't know where I stood on using training tools.

Honestly, I stood nowhere.

I had met people who used e-collars on their dogs. In both instances, they were well-behaved and happy dogs that Jace had played with on several occasions. One, the owner explained her dog had reactivity toward mail carriers (not kidding), and the other told us sometimes his boy played rough and had to be recalled.

At that point I didn't even know there were different types of training.

What I quickly discovered was my current trainer was considered a *positive reinforcement* (R+) trainer—a method also known as purely positive (PP) or force free (FF).

I was now learning about *balanced training*, a rewards-based training method that also implements corrections in the training process to prevent unwanted or dangerous behaviours. Balanced trainers believe in using tools—such as e-collars and prong collars—where needed, under guidance of an experienced user.

There were also other methods, including *least intrusive, minimally aversive* (LIMA), which is sort of between R+ and balanced training, and on the opposite end of the spectrum, a negative reinforcement and punishment-based method called *compulsion* training.

When Jess explained how much an e-collar had helped her and her dog Iorveth, I began to do my own research on what balanced training and the use of tools like the e-collar really looked like. I started watching YouTube videos by Tom Davis, Sean O'Shea and Jamie Penrith. I bought Larry Krohn's e-collar book and followed Ted Efthymiadis of Mango Dog.

I'd never thought of the e-collar as a bad thing, I just never considered it for a fearful dog—a dog like Jace.

Month 34: Pharmaceutical Bonanza

STARTING ON AUGUST 1ST, under guidance of our vet and the vet behaviourist we came up with a program of medications; it ended up being a cocktail of 12 pills per day.

Clonidine (1x twice daily): used for treating certain behavioural disorders in dogs such as phobias, aggression, and separation anxiety.

Fluoxetine (2x once daily in the morning): also known as Prozac these are selective serotonin reuptake inhibitors (SSRI) and used to combat anxiety.

Apo Gabapentin (3x twice daily): used to treat anxiety and believed to inhibit the release of excitatory neurotransmitters.

Alprazolam (1x twice daily): a fast working non-cumulative tranquilizer commonly used as quick acting anti-anxiety drug.

That many meds concerned me, what were they doing to his body?

However, our goal was only a year of the concoction. This meant once those meds kicked in, in about 8 weeks, I had to figure out a way to work on Jace's fears, starting with getting him to go outside and pee.

In the interim I worked up the courage to talk to Barry about training Jace with an e-collar. I didn't know how it would look, I mean, I had done my research, but still felt I was in over my head. Nagging fears I'd screw Jace up worse than he already was continued to plague me—but I also realized I had no choice.

Barry reluctantly agreed after I pled my case, and shared the research I had done.

We decided to order an Educator EZ-900 two-dog system package, which came with one transmitter, two receivers and two biothane collars. As per Jess's advice, we ordered backup biothane bungee collars—to allow for more range of movement—and comfort pads, which were the contact points between dog's neck and the receiver. In a hairless dog, the softly rounded tips of the comfort pads were a must.

At that point, I had no real expectation of using the second collar on Xoco, but I wanted the option.

> The *E* in e-collar stands for electronic. They are a fantastic means of communication—the version I purchased had a half-mile radius, 100 levels of stimulation and multiple modes for vibration and tone. They are not *shock* collars.

Something I will ever be grateful for was Jess's honest advice, and her suggestion to start keeping a diary of Jace's progression

Month 35: Waiting for a Miracle

ON SEPTEMBER 15TH we had a follow up visit with the vet behaviourist.

While the Alprazolam (the non-cumulative fast acting tranquilizer) seemed to be chilling Jace out enough to go pee with less struggle—note, I say *less*—it made him dozy, and when we did take him to the beach to run off-leash, he had little energy or enthusiasm.

This bothered us deeply,

While the meds seemed to loosen him up, not much changed—his behaviour and willingness to go outside was still dependant on the time of day, the environment, and the weather.

During her second visit I told the vet behaviourist I had bought an e-collar and intended to use it for recall purposes—because that was the plan.

Being anti-tool, she didn't applaud the decision, but did agree in Jace's case for recall it could be a good idea.

After doing what I thought was a comprehensive search for a suitable balanced trainer in Vancouver, I came up empty handed. I still wanted help with conditioning Jace to the e-collar.

I asked Jess if she knew of anyone close by.

She in turn reached out to her trainer Rachel, and asked if she knew of anyone. Rachel knew only one, a trainer on Vancouver Island.

On September 17th I reached out to the balanced trainer on Vancouver Island. Filling out the consult request form on her website, I told her Jace's entire story. I hoped she would be willing to train me on the e-collar during one of her visits to the mainland. Unfortunately the next day she replied that based on my information, Jace needed full rehabilitation and she wouldn't take on a case like his except for a minimum two-week board and train.

While I understood her response, it was hard pass. Jace would not be going anywhere; I just wasn't prepared to part with him when he was already so fragile.

We were back at square one, and while Jace was drugged enough to sometimes go out to pee, he was willing to do little else. He refused to poop except for first thing in the morning under the cover of darkness, which had become his crutch.

It had been six weeks since we started him on his cocktail of meds and I was seeing no change in his anxiety.

After weeks of looking at the e-collar in its box I finally opened it up; I watched a few YouTube videos on programming the collar and set it up. The next step was putting it on Jace. Initially I put it on him while he was in the house doing his daily dog stuff, without turning it on.

Then after following Larry Krohn's book *Everything You Need To Know About E Collar Training,* and studying videos of all the other trainers I'd come to rely upon, I turned it on and tested it on myself—on my inner wrist. I couldn't feel it until the pulse—or *muscle stimulation*—was at number 14 out of 100. I then put the collar back on Jace and found his working level.

> The working level on an e-collar is the first sign your dog feels the stim. It might let you know by a simple flick of an ear, or a glance in your direction. Start at level one when finding your dog's working level—each dog differs.

It's important to note Educator e-collars have 100 levels—they are not cheap pet store versions with a handful of levels.

Jace noticed the pulse at level four. To this day I call his working level a four or five.

Over the course of several days, I trained him with tone and stim simultaneously. The tone was incredibly important to me, because I wanted it to be the main use of the collar.

I trained Jace to *come to me* with tone. I trained him to *come to me* using working level stim. I trained him to *come with me* using tone, and *come with me* using working level stim. This was all done rewards-based with high value treats such as: cheese, boiled chicken, or sausage.

Looking back, I realized we had never properly trained Jace on *come* pre-e-collar, he would come when we called while inside, but we'd never done any proper training outdoors, a big part of that was we never expected to have him off-leash.

It was extremely poor judgment and inexcusable inexperience.

It's very important to clarify once again, if you decide to start using an e-collar, pay up for a professional high quality product. Remember, it's a tool to communicate with your dog, not punish it!

Speak to a professional, do your research, please make sure you are doing things correctly!

The e-collar is not meant only for correction—I can't underline that enough.

It is a tool for communication.

Not being a trainer I feel it's irresponsible of me to get into the minutiae of how I began conditioning and training Jace with the e-collar, but suffice it to say I did it slowly, and with plenty of positive reinforcement.

What I can say, and this is crucial—the first time I took Jace outside with the e-collar on was to go for a pee. I put on his leash, I said *come* and hit the tone button, and he followed me into the lane with no leash pressure.

For the first time since we'd moved to our new home he just followed me. No hesitation, and no drama about the environment—zero fight.

We didn't need a miracle, we had just communicated. I told him what I wanted him to do, and he understood.

Sun worshippers

Month 36:
Learning to Trust the Tools

ON OCTOBER 1ST I had what was to be the last session with our R+ trainer for Xoco. It was pretty much to get her on-leash walking in check. She'd begun pulling and stopping to sniff everything; I was frustrated and felt I could do with some help.

I told her I had started using an e-collar on Jace for recall purposes and to my surprise she understood. She told me she had used an e-collar on her previous dog, that in order for to it have off-leash freedom, she needed to.

She said she would like to guide me on how to use it, but if she did there was a chance she could lose her license.

What I didn't tell her, was due to two separate recent incidences, where Jace was acting combatively toward another dog for no apparent reason—there was zero correlation between those two dogs as one was off-leash and the other on-leash—we decided that until Jace was in a more neutral state of mind we did not intend to let him play with other dogs.

It was a painful decision but we felt the risk was too high.

We were now eight weeks into Jace's meds and I prayed we'd start seeing changes in his behaviour any day.

Instead he continued to mess in the house, so I purchased male dog diapers.

I put them on him each time he was out of my sight. Even so, if I were gone for a longer time, for a run, or to take Xoco on a walk, he would pee in the diaper.

It was better than the floor, but it was still upsetting.

On the morning of October 6th we were out on the tidal flats with both dogs and Jace started trotting toward and barking at a couple of beachcombers. I used the tone on the e-collar, which he ignored, then said come at a level six with the stim—he promptly returned.

I was impressed with how quickly it worked—I was seeing more benefits from the e-collar.

I used it at slightly higher level on October 17th to call him away from two Golden Retrievers playing on the beach not far from us.

October 22nd was my first zoom session with Jess's balanced trainer from Washington State. Rachel was the owner of On The Mark Balanced Training.

When I couldn't find someone to help us locally, she agreed to work with me virtually. A lot of that first conversation was about Jace's background and what I was hoping to achieve.

Rachel tried to instill in me the importance of using the e-collar for more than just recall, that we needed to use it for structure and correction for other undesirable behaviours such as whining and barking. Both of those types of behaviours build anxiety in a dog—a dog such as Jace—one already teeming with stress that didn't need more. A calm state of mind was our goal.

I heard what she was saying but I was still stuck on the immediate; what we desperately needed to address first: going outside to pee, and recall.

With her guidance, I did start using it to train Jace on *place*, however inconsistently.

> *Place* refers to a spot such as a raised cot or dog bed, where the dog remains in a relaxed down for portions of the day. I.E., when you are: cooking dinner, working, housework, or when guests are visiting.

Place creates a calm mind and space for the dog, but when first learning they generally try to move from *place*, which you can correct using the e-collar.

Barry wasn't happy with this additional use of the tool at all. We had made a deal, the e-collar was for use on recall only; I felt stuck between progress and household harmony.

What did immediately benefit us was Rachel's recommendation to use a slip lead.

To be clear, since we'd moved homes, Jace did not walk on leash anywhere, except in very specific circumstances.

He would however, now walk to the nearby garage where we parked our car, so I no longer had to drive it right up to our gate.

To him, the risk of walking to the car was worth the reward of going to the beach and being off-leash.

Jace now associated the car with freedom.

Once we arrived at the beach he would then walk from the car to the shore.

He would not walk left nor right once we arrived at our destination, only directly to the source of his reward.

Rewards were: car→beach, car→home.

In those moments he would literally drag me. His fear of everything in between the car and the house, or the car and the beach, made him panic and pull toward his goal.

His back would concave, his tail would tuck right under his belly and his entire body would get low to the ground—it resembled a crawl.

When I put the slip lead Rachel recommended on him for the first time, it relieved a significant part of his pulling.

> When applied properly, slip leads can apply pressure or tighten when tension is applied, such as when a dog pulls. They release pressure or loosen when the tension is gone, i.e. when the dog stops pulling.

Jace was no longer able to use his upper body strength to haul me as he could with a flat collar or a harness—and I no longer had to worry about his trachea collapsing from fear pulling.

But we were at another crossroad.

The summer tidal flats had all but disappeared, which meant no off-leash time unless we arrived to the much smaller Spanish Banks off-leash dog beach as early as possible. Sometimes we were lucky enough to have moments of free time, while watching for approaching dogs.

Thanks to our recent successes I decided to take Jace off the Alprazolam on October 25th.

The drugs were not doing what I had hoped; our new training however was beginning to really give us traction.

I do not recommend taking your dog off any medication without consulting your vet, but because the Alprazolam was a non-cumulative tranquilizer, I knew I wouldn't mess up the rest of his meds. I felt strongly at that point that particular drug was making him dopey and I didn't like seeing him that way any more than he liked feeling that way.

Additionally I wanted to see how it would affect his behaviour. Would removing it from his system send our progress backward, or was the training what was truly helping?

As I suspected, he did not backslide.

We had one last low tide of the year on the 25th to let the dogs run free—and took it. But of course, things can always go wrong. An off-leash Pomeranian bolted toward us across the flats, as its oblivious owner wandered in the opposite direction more than a city block's distance away.

I made an error that day I've learned not to repeat in those situations.

Seeing that dog rocketing toward us, I began yelling to the owner to recall her dog. She was too far away to hear me. Instead all I did was alert Jace (and Xoco) of the incoming fur ball, and Jace went right after it, Xoco in his wake.

He was running at the dog in an threatening manner—his body language obvious: stiff, low to the ground and taut upright tail—while Xoco thought she was going to get to play. I was calling him while rolling the dial up on the e-collar stim; even in the high 60s he blew me off. Jace rolled the dog, it yelped, and ran off.

By the time he returned and my heart slowed down fractionally, I'd realized two things.

One, pulling him away from off-leash play with other dogs was still the best choice for now. Two, we needed to get Xoco properly trained on the e-collar as well. Even if she was only along for the ride as she chased behind him, I had to get her sorted, stat.

I didn't want to breed pack mentality.

Having two dogs not under control was not only irresponsible, but also extraordinarily dangerous for them.

Dressing for Dia de Los Muertos. The Author with Xoco and Jace. Photo: Barry Komar

PART 6
Month 37: Sniffari

IN HOPES OF BUILDING Jace's confidence, and solidifying our relationship, I signed him up for nose work (scent work) classes each Sunday for six weeks.

On November 9th we attended our first K9 Nose Works class at a training facility in South Vancouver.

While the six human owners sat distanced from each inside the facility, our dogs stayed in their respective cars until it was their turn.

I honestly wasn't even sure I could get Jace into the building to participate and expressed my concerns to the instructor, who was sympathetic.

As the owners introduced themselves and told a little about each of their dogs, I noted that several mentioned their dog was anxious, and of course each had its quirks.

I recall thinking; just wait until you meet Jace.

Sure enough, dog after dog came in and had their first *run*—they all seemed confident to me, after all, I lived with true fear.

When Jace came in I could sense the collective shock. His panting and tucked tail, whining, pacing and panic were startling, and likely beyond what they'd ever seen.

Yet he came in. He vacillated between moments of curiosity and alarm, but he did participate in a vague sort of way.

It was still a win in my books. And each Sunday, he would dance around in nervous excitement wanting to be involved but something in his brain was holding him back from engaging fully in the exercise.

> Nose work is a human/dog team sport. While the dog does the majority of work, it's a partnership. In novice sessions, if your dog can't quite get to, or find a hidden scent/treat, you assist, and still reward them for finding it.

We primarily used boxes of different sizes and hid treats inside. Awareness of your dog's limitations in those early stages was important. I knew, for example, Jace wasn't going to stick his head into a small space, so treats went into large shallow boxes.

It's common sense to set your dog up for success—and that became my mantra not only for Jace, but Xoco.

Ultimately nose work became routine in our home with both dogs. Especially when I realized what an awesome way it was to stimulate and exercise them on poor weather days; they absolutely adored it.

That same second weekend of November we started pushing Jace's boundaries a little more.

I began parking the car a little farther from the dog beach, forcing him to actually walk there on leash. It was extremely beneficial when, thanks to COVID, and anti-gathering protocols, Vancouver Parks Board locked down all parking lots around the off-leash dog area at Spanish Banks. We had no choice but to walk.

On November 10th, my second session with Rachel, I made sure to time it so Barry could join in. I needed her to make him understand the importance of using the e-collar in all aspects of Jace's life. I was beginning to grasp how comprehensively it could be used—thanks to her guidance and that of other professional trainers I was following on Instagram.

She was able to alleviate Barry's fears that using the e-collar for more than just recall would not confuse or harm him when used correctly.

With Rachel's tutelage, we started practicing *downs* in locations other than his *place* by working with light leash pressure for direction, and his working level on the e-collar.

We were noticing some minor behavioural changes in him; specifically he was slightly less reactive, barking at fewer at dogs walking past our home when he could see them through the window.

To be honest though, I still wasn't following through on much of what Rachel advised. Mostly because I couldn't see immediate improvements like I could with stuff we worked on outdoors.

Aspects of e-collar use indoors remained intimidating, and unnecessary to me.

Outside however, with the slip lead to prevent pulling, and correcting reactivity with the e-collar—when Jace fixated on another dog I wanted to immediately correct the fixation, rather than waiting for the explosion/reaction to happen—we were making progress.

That evolution included walking from one end of Spanish Banks to the other and back; but that only worked on early morning walks when it was quiet and there were very few distractions. If we tried to walk him along the shoreline path during daylight hours with all the people about, he'd melt down.

When we did come across other dogs on those mornings, I took a wide berth and would attempt to correct him for fixating.

I was still stiff using the transmitter, I didn't yet have the fluidity for maximum effect, and I would tense up whenever I saw another dog. While my adeptness with the transmitter would improve over time and consistency, I also needed my body language to relax for his benefit. Regardless of my awkward handling he was still improving, and in some situations he'd go many days without a reaction.

Despite this I vacillated between knowing he would never improve if we didn't cross paths with other dogs often enough, and being highly relieved when we didn't.

Winter white. Xolos fade without sunlight.

Month 38: Need to Evacuate

WHILE PROGRESS CRAWLED, I still felt huge relief at getting Jace a fraction more exercise in the form of those weekend morning beach walks.

Getting him to heel on those walks like I needed continued to be frustrating.

I was wholly aware the point of a tight heel walk was to keep Jace with his head parallel with my hip.

In that position he could see me in his periphery and move with me.

The goal was to pull him out of the lead where he was vulnerable, that in fact I was his leader, there to protect him. All he needed to do was follow my lead.

Sadly I had to admit while Jace might love me, but he didn't trust me to protect him.

And I was still soft on the e-collar.

Jace, in his constant state of high arousal, needed a higher correction than I was giving him; even when I did, I didn't feel I getting through to him with consistency.

It was verbal diarrhoea from me: *heel, heel, heel...*

His body was beside mine—just farther ahead than our trainer Rachel wanted to see.

In addition there was the ongoing issue of the weekday poops.

If his morning constitutionals were interrupted—the paper delivery person startling him, or the neighbour's cat running across the lane, Jace just wouldn't go. And because he refused to walk on busy weekdays at the beach, he was going days without pooping; or he'd do it in the house when I turned my back.

We needed to find an alternative daytime walk, somewhere quiet that we could also be legally off-leash.

Acadia Beach was our saviour.

Just around the corner from Spanish Banks, Acadia's off-leash stony beach came complete with a parking lot so we could access it easily. There were often dogs there, but not like the busy sandy beach at Spanish Banks' off-leash park. It was generally quiet all day and we could see a good distance in case we had to leash up.

It wasn't fun to walk on, being comprised primarily of saucer sized and larger alluvial stones, but it got us out during the week for fresh air, activity and the ever-important evacuations Jace needed.

It also gave him much-needed moments of just being a dog, sniffing and playing with Xoco.

Underscoring our decision to stop off-leash socialization was one Sunday morning at Spanish Banks. A friendly Toller Jace used to play with unexpectedly came onto the beach at least 50 meters away.

Seemingly in slow motion, I called to Jace to come and hit the tone button on the transmitter; he ignored me and ran directly away from me down the shore at the Toller. Xoco was on his heels, again.

I was hitting the stim and rolling the dial. I could hear Jace yelping but he blew me off, and he scared the hell out of the much smaller Toller.

Luckily the owners were chill about it, they were close to the scene and said Jace was just establishing dominance.

I didn't care what it looked like, it was wrong and it was scary.

Similar to the incident with the Pomeranian in October, Xoco was thinking she was going to get to play with a new dog; Jace was being an ass.

In the off-leash area at Spanish Banks during low tide, wearing e-collars. Photo: Barry Komar

Month 39-43: The Doldrums

WHY IT TOOK SO bloody long to buy another crate I'll never know. Maybe we were holding out for the meds to kick in. The reality was we were five months in and the only progression I felt that had been made was thanks to training.

By the end of January Jace had another crate, an exact replica of Xoco's, positioned side-by-side with hers.

He hadn't had a crate for almost two and a half years, back to a time when we'd lived in our former home.

It was sometime in the summer of 2018 he showed us he was a big boy and could be left to wander freely in our bedroom behind a dog gate, and we'd trusted him. It was also nice to have that big ugly crate gone, as small as our bedroom was.

But with all the separation anxiety and messing in the house for more than half a year, it was time.

I switched his *place* to his crate, just as Xoco's crate was hers.

When in *place,* which honestly still wasn't often or consistent, the door was open.

When I went for a run, or to take Xoco out—because let's be honest, I wasn't going anywhere else working from home during a pandemic—for a walk, his crate door was locked.

Even if I was taking out the garbage, he was crated.

It was such a huge relief I still shake my head as to why we had dragged our feet so long, especially because Xoco had been happily crated since she arrived.

In part it was for her safety as a puppy. I wasn't going to leave Jace alone with her in the beginning, and the crate stayed because she loved it—it was her den.

Somehow, Xoco lost her e-collar/receiver on the beach on December 31st so we purchased a new one for her in early January; it was an Educator EZ-400 kit with a new receiver and transmitter. Using the EZ-900 two-dog system (one transmitter with two receivers) we already had was great in theory but not in reality since Barry was generally the one walking her when we four were out.

So we now had separate transmitters.

Xoco also had a habit of amping Jace up, when other dogs were in the vicinity, she was excited and would whine over wanting to meet on-leash; meanwhile I was trying to keep Jace tranquil, and away from other dogs.

Yes, we made the mistake of on-leash greetings when she was a puppy. In hindsight, another lesson learned. She never developed leash reactivity, but could have; I'd seen it happen. Avoiding on-leash greetings in a city of dogs seemed almost impossible, so I didn't beat myself up over it.

It was up to Barry to keep Xoco calm and sometimes he would let her off-leash to play with another dog while Jace and I sat away from the beach to observe.

However, Xoco's recall training was all my doing, so if he pressed the tone to come, she would return to me, even when he voiced the command. That's fine in most cases, but not while she was playing with another pup, and in giving chase would follow her directly to me, and Jace.

We stopped doing that around the same time I realized I didn't want her playing with off-leash dogs I didn't know anymore. Fewer good play experiences were far better than a lot of poor ones—and much safer.

I signed Jace up for a second series of nose work classes and took Xoco too.

They would vie to get out of the car when I would come to collect one for a run. I loved Jace's enthusiasm, even if he sort of froze up once we got inside the facility for his turn.

After that I took Xoco to agility classes solo—no surprise, she excelled.

She was exactly the puppy we hoped she would be. Outgoing and confidant, joyful, and quite biddable as far as Xolos go. I started calling her the Teflon Xolo—where the breed is naturally skittish, she was a sassy and assured little monkey—the complete opposite of Jace in many ways.

She still had classic Xolo traits: high prey drive, independent, environmentally aware, and quick to alert you of possible danger.

But she was also less aloof than a lot of her kind, and more accepting of direction than many—perhaps the result of the relationship I cultivated with her from day one. Like others of her breed she was quick to learn and very intelligent, but also sensitive. Xolos do not like reprimands and raised voices.

Over the next few months life became routine.

Twice a week we would go to Acadia beach when Barry returned from work; since his day began at 5 a.m., and finished by 2 p.m., we always had a good portion of the afternoons free. On the weekends we would continue our long morning walks along Spanish Banks. Jace didn't really improve, but he wasn't backsliding. His reactivity was still swift and quite consistent to nearby dogs.

I'm not proud to say, but one of my biggest concerns during this time was hiding the e-collars from others, and especially our growing Instagram followers.

The crux was insecurity on my part; I was using a tool I never seemed to see on any other dogs, and I still lacked certainty in my training abilities.

At first hiding those tools was easy, winter clothing and snoods were on every day, so the e-collars remained hidden. That changed in April, when frolicking in their natural nakedness at the beach was once again possible, and the e-collars were highly visible.

And with the warmer weather the low tides returned so I would often take both dogs to the beach myself. I had confidence in Xoco's recall, and kept keep plenty of distance from others.

At that point I figured we were getting about as much out of Jace as we could. My apathy was okay—until it wasn't.

I wasn't trying hard enough. I still wasn't creating the structure I'd been advised I needed, nor was I pushing Jace's boundaries enough.

JACE'S JOURNEY

Back to bronze for the summer

PART 7
Month 44: Be the Change

I GENUINELY CANNOT SAY what prompted my next steps; perhaps I was tired of the plateau we slogged along on?

On June 1st I finally started to make desperately needed changes.

It was called rehabilitation; I just didn't know it yet.

I built structure and pattern into our days, starting with the simplest of additions to our routine.

Each time I took Jace out for a pee, I had him sit in our lane and just watch.

He struggled at first, physically and mentally; he was so used to dragging me back to our yard.

Making him sit and be calm in an environment he wanted to escape from challenged him, but repetition was key.

At least three times per day we did this, just five minutes of sitting and observing the leaves rustle in the trees, reflections on neighbouring windows, people pushing strollers, and cyclists passing. While our lane was extremely quiet, there was still enough traffic to make him skittish.

If he tried to pull me back to the house, or broke from his sit, I used the e-collar to correct him. Low numbers, higher than his indoor working level because he was of course in a higher state of arousal, but just enough to remind him he needed to stay put.

He desperately needed to be challenged.

After a couple days, I started putting him in a down. It's a more vulnerable position, but it was also designed to create a calmer mindset.

He needed to trust I would be there to protect him.

Many trainers believe a dog is calmer in down, as a sit is calmer than a stand. I was fully aware just having him in a down wasn't a miracle cure that he would suddenly be serene in that position, but it was still beneficial.

In a few places within sight of our home I would move Jace, doing down-stays with consistency but mixing it up so he didn't always have the same view.

I was extremely careful however. I didn't want a dog, or something else that could backfire on us, startle him in those early days.

Success breeds success.

On June 5th I was able to get Jace to walk halfway down our lane. I used the tone to *come with me* as I had trained him. When he panicked and froze I wouldn't let him pull me toward home, I would stop, have him sit, and just be, to observe, for a minute.

He needed to understand I wasn't dragging him forward, but also that he wasn't allowed to drag me back. This again was my way of telling him I understood he was scared and I wasn't forcing him, but I also wasn't going to let him run back to safety.

He needed to trust me.

The very next morning Jace walked with me around the entire block. Let me repeat: he walked around our entire block!

I cannot express enough what a monumental turning point that was.

It wasn't just a breakthrough; it was knocking the bloody wall down.

We continued those walks around the block in the quiet mornings. We'd made a lot of progress; I wasn't going to send Jace spinning out of control by pushing him out there during busy parts of the day, yet.

We did it at our pace, which by a lot of standards was slow, but I wasn't taking any chances with his mental health.

Still struggling with explosive reactivity the few times Jace was coming across other dogs—especially near our home where he was especially territorial—I did something I never expected to do.

I ordered a Herm-Sprenger prong collar.

Before you slam down this book or toss it in the trash, hear me out.

Yes, I knew prong collars looked barbaric. Yes, I was fully aware my dog had no fur to protect him, but I did my homework. I researched its use and why it was designed to be a much safer collar to use on dogs that pull.

Made in Germany, Herm-Sprenger designs many products for dogs including the prong (or training) collar. A simple looking but beautifully engineered collar, it applies equal pressure all around the dog's neck rather than putting pressure primarily at the trachea. I continued to be concerned Jace would hurt himself (or me) and I needed a solution so we could keep up the momentum of his new walking, while significantly reducing the impact of his lunging.

> Prong collars are engineered to apply equal pressure around the neck rather than putting pressure directly on the trachea, causing possible damage to dogs prone to pulling.

I spoke to other Xolo owners who used the collars and discovered they'd had no issues with prongs damaging skin; just in case I also bought rubber tips to place on each prong.

The change was immediate, I needed a fraction of leash pressure when correcting/directing him than with the slip lead—it helped his heel immensely.

I invite you to research these collars yourself to fully understand their use, proper application, purpose, and amazing function.

On June 20th we began extending the morning walks to Granville Island.

Jace was already used to our short morning path, so getting him to continue his walk, farther away from his home safety zone resulted in small struggles. Using tone on the e-collar was enough to pull him out of his compulsion and follow me.

We made it all the way to the Kitsilano off-leash dog beach, about two kilometres west of us, on the morning of June 27th.

At this point I knew I'd had solidified Jace's trust and he was willing to follow me anywhere within reason.

I did not take advantage of his faith in me. Everything I asked of him he was capable of, and I took great care to continue to make him feel safe.

I truly felt it was the way a dog like him needed to be handled: with firm guidance, trust and safety, and at a pace he could sustain without pushing him over his threshold.

For four years—his entire life—Jace had lived his life in fear. I wasn't going to be overly ambitious and damage our relationship. He was still a fragile dog, maybe not as much as he would like people to think, but I knew he still needed to be handled with care.

Month 45: Not Giving Up

JULY'S PROGRESSION INCLUDED CONTINUED longer weekend walks. It was a huge relief knowing we didn't have to drive to Spanish Banks to get him to walk anymore.

I added night walks to the mix. Generally the last pee of the night was a quick step outside to relieve himself; but evenings were a peaceful time of day and I wanted to keep the momentum going, so I added in that second walk.

Jace's heel continued improving around that time. I didn't have to hound him and constantly use the e-collar to keep him close to me. His head wasn't exactly where I wanted it, he was slightly forward, but I could feel him finally getting it.

Those walks progressed to mid-day when the seawall was busy.

Jace really struggled with those walks, but as part of his desensitization process I felt we needed to move forward.

About the same time I started putting him in a down-stay on a bench off to one side of the seawall where there was plenty of space. It was a new vantage point for him; he shook and panted, and his head would with ping-pong back and forth as people would wander past.

From my research I felt strongly coddling his fears was something to avoid. Hugging or babying a dog that is fearful just encourages the behaviour; it makes them believe there really is something to be fearful of.

But Jace's entire being just seemed in chaos in those moments. I wondered if a hand on his back, a reassurance was okay. I did so sometimes to see if it would calm him, versus just sitting there beside him quietly. The impact was minimal, but I still felt the odd touch, no words, just a little comfort was worth it.

I wanted to talk to someone with more experience on the matter.

My trainer Rachel referred me to someone she had shadowed, head trainer Josh from Julie's K9 Academy in Maryland. Josh specialized in behaviour modification and rehabilitation.

In preparation, I had Barry take videos of me walking Jace around the seawall during the busy mid-day. Looking at that video afterward was an eye-opener—it hit me hard. I only ever looked at Jace from above as we walked.

In the primary video he almost slinked, his tail tucked right under his belly.

I knew we had a long way to go; I knew consistency was key. I just felt I needed more help.

I sent the videos off to Josh to view before our July 29th session.

A couple hours beforehand, I received a message via Instagram, that after viewing the videos, they felt Jace's issues were too considerable; that a video chat was not appropriate for his case—I needed a professional hands-on trainer who knew how to rehabilitate dogs. They told me they would have to cancel, that the severity of Jace's case was too extreme for a virtual session.

I was utterly crushed. I felt so strongly that an opportunity to chat with Josh—whom I had been following on Instagram and YouTube—would be exactly the next step we needed.

I plead my case.

I told them we had no balanced trainers in our vicinity, and a previous trainer had already given up on us.

They responded that Josh's methods were far too advanced for the average owner; even professional trainers he did video chats with often had a hard time keeping up with him.

I tried once more with these exact words, "Say I'm not an average owner? I just took a weekend long dog psychology and behaviour course last weekend, so I'm willing to put in the time. I know that's not much compared to an actual trainer (I actually looked into doing that [becoming a trainer] as well, but with COVID it's nearly impossible) but I'm not going to give up on him."

Minutes later I got a response.

"Okay, he says he'll do it!"

Barry joined in on the meeting—I felt it was a crucial session.

Excitement and nervousness set in. I was going to meet a trainer I followed and respected. Since delving into dog training deeper, I was thoroughly fascinated by it and loved listening to people with a momentous amount of experience.

The breed fascinated Josh, who had never heard of a Xoloitzcuintli. He studied our videos and noted while Jace was anxious he was also curious, which was important. He agreed we couldn't correct Jace for his constant surveillance every time he swivelled to look at a possible threat. I was relieved because I hadn't been doing that, unless it was a fixation on a dog, which could lead to a reaction.

For the most part Jace didn't fixate on other dogs during those high-arousal walks; competing stimuli surrounded us and divided his attention.

When walking, Jace was rarely at ease enough to just be a dog, sniff, and do doggie things, so I kept him in a tight heel until I felt he might be relaxed enough to do so. Josh agreed even in a tight heel if Jace wanted to sniff to let him—it was a positive message he was sending and I needed to encourage that.

Luckily I had sat in on many of Josh's live Instagram sessions and I muddled through when he spoke about rehabilitation and some of the techniques he used.

At the end of the session, I knew Jace and I were on the right path, Josh was right when he said there was no hurry; we were working at our own speed. He also said what I had done with Jace so far was remarkable; he had trained trainers who wouldn't have gotten as far as I had, and to reach out if I ever needed help.

Just a week before my session with Josh I had completed a two-day dog psychology and behaviour modification seminar with trainer and breeder based in Kamloops, B.C.

During those two days I came to realize I'd picked up a lot of information on my own over the past 11 months; I learned little from the course, which was disappointing based on how much I paid.

But I was relieved, buoyed and ready to keep facing challenges with my boy after a mere 75-minute discussion with Josh.

July also brought outdoor training sessions in our yard.

Movements in our lane were triggers. Xoco would get excited when people walked by, and if it were a dog, she was right up against the gate on her hind legs wanting to say hi. Jace would warn people away and he was becoming notorious for his aggressive territorial behaviour toward other canines.

I was tired of both of their behaviours, so I started the sessions with me relaxing in a lawn chair and them in down-stays on *place* on cushions. I would keep both remotes in my hand and correct them for getting out of place, or any verbal drama.

The goal was neutrality as life went on outside the gate.

It was very effective, and led to me practicing threshold work with them.

With them in a down-stay just inside the open front door, I would walk out our gate and away from the house, first staying in sight and then progressing farther away, eventually completely out of sight. Each time they stayed in place I would return and treat.

If I was in sight and could see one or both break place, I could quickly correct.

If I wasn't in sight and couldn't see, I couldn't correct, but I could still refrain from treating when I returned to them; then we'd practice it again.

I knew thresholds were important for dogs to understand.

They were not allowed to breach a doorway—that barrier—unless I said.

Waiting for permission was not only respectful but also safe.

It was my job as a responsible owner to train our dogs; that included not rushing people who came to the door, or darting out the gate, possibly getting hit by a car.

JACE'S JOURNEY

Photo: Barry Komar

Photo: Barry Komar

Month 46: Nailed it!

SINCE JACE BECAME OURS he had never had his nails trimmed.

It sounded ludicrous, but nail management was a real issue with so many dogs.

I had tried to clip his nails in the first months we got him. I managed to do a couple of them once or twice, then I clipped one a little too short; he yelped, it bled.

That was it.

At age two we took him to a groomer. I watched as the groomer tried to clip them, Jace is amazingly strong and wriggly when he wants to be. It was horrible seeing him trying to pin Jace on the ground as we stood by. I finally said just stop; the relieved groomer gave up.

The vet was our next option. Our family vet and three assistants could not hold him down. We opted to put him under to get the job done.

That was a one-time solution. It was not something I wanted to continue; it was too stressful, and not sustainable.

A scratchboard with sandpaper glued to it did a decent job on his front nails for the next couple years, but it left his dewclaws and back claws untouched.

On August 2nd I started desensitizing Jace to the Dremel nail grinder. We'd had it for years, but had even less luck with the grinder than the clippers.

Touching and massaging Jace's paws had never been an issue— so I started there.

For five minutes every second day I would have him in a down on his side, hold his paws, talk gently, and introduce the Dremel.

He wore the e-collar during this desensitization process and I did have it set on his working level.

I would place the device on the ground near him while holding a paw and mark the moment with a "good" while passing him a high quality treat. I slowly moved on to turning the Dremel on, setting it nearby and holding a paw (marking with a good/treat). Holding the Dremel turned off against a paw came next (good/treat). Eventually I was able to turn on the Dremel and hold the base against a paw so he could feel the vibration (good/treat).

That last step was difficult, and I had to be firm with him. If he tried to bolt from his down I'd use the e-collar to correct him.

> Short but frequent sessions with plenty of high quality treats works best when desensitizing a dog to a nail grinder. Try five minutes or less per day or every second day. It may take weeks, but it's worth it.

Many people would disagree with the use of the e-collar for introducing nail work, but after four years, I needed to show Jace he couldn't decide to just up and walk away from me. He'd been running from his fears his entire life and I'd allowed it.

It worked. Three weeks later I was grinding down nails on all four of Jace's paws three times per week, without use of the e-collar at all.

The point being, Jace trusted me after those weeks, he didn't love getting his nails groomed but he knew it wasn't hurting him.

It was a means to an end.

August also meant we had passed the one-year mark since Jace had been on his cocktail of medications. I reached out to his vet and the vet behaviourist explaining Jace's progress and requesting we start to wean him off.

On August 10th the Apo Gabapentin went first.

We reduced the quantity and doses over three weeks until he was completely off that drug. We decided to wait a couple months before weaning him off the Clonidine.

With Jace's new lease on life and frequent walks I was beginning to notice something I'd only vaguely been aware of before.

Vancouver had an epidemic; it was called off-leash dogs.

While I'd heard people complain about the volume of illegally off-leash dogs around the city I only began to consider their proliferation once I needed to advocate for Jace and earn his trust; confidence I'd been building for months.

My frustration and anger grew the more of them I crossed paths with. They seemed to be multiplying. The problem was very few of those dogs were well trained enough to be off-leash in an off-leash park let alone on a sidewalk or pathway. It resulted in normalizing off-leash dogs—new dog owners seeing other dogs off-leash made it seem okay. My dog is friendly; why not let her/him off too?

Ergo, more and more dogs off-leash.

Irresponsible dog owners were everywhere. Distracted by cell phones or conversations with others, dogs were pooping on private and public lawns without the owner seeing it happen. Equally, off-leash dogs were running amok, creating reactivity in on-leash dogs.

When I would confront these thoughtless owners, they would blame me. According to them, my dog was the problem and he should be locked up, their dog was not the problem—their dog was friendly.

It was something that shouldn't have been up for discussion period; they were all in the wrong because there were laws being broken everywhere. There seemed to be zero follow through from the city, and no one around handing out fines.

Off-leash dog owners were a selfish bunch. My dog's mental health had no bearing on their decision. Their ignorance made my brain hurt, they had no care that my dog being tethered while their free dog approached was dangerous to all parties involved.

Then something dreadful happened a mere block from our home.

We were told a small off-leash dog (known for being off-leash) ran up to two on-leash dogs with intent. The on-leash dogs retaliated causing significant injury to the small dog, which resulted in that dog spending hours in surgery.

Unfortunately, despite vet care it later died of its injuries.

The owner of the off-leash dog was not only stuck with what I can imagine was a massive vet bill but also fined $5000 by the city for being in the wrong.

What a tragic way to learn a lesson.

Yet that owner, or a sympathizer, started posting signs all over our neighbourhood claiming two dangerous pit-bull type dogs had killed a nine-pound Yorkie and if you saw them to alert animal control. That threw Barry and I into indignation. We walked our two dogs around that route all the time, what if someone pointed at us thinking it was our duo—suddenly everyone was whispering about two dangerous dogs roaming around. Not one person we spoke to considered where the blame really rested. Luckily the signs had all disappeared within a few days.

Consider how the owner of the two appropriately leashed dogs felt, what that owner had to live with.

PART 8

Month 47: Pepper Spray & First Aid

AFTER SIX MONTHS OF some epic off-leash beach time, we knew our season of low tides was ending, so we embraced those fleeting days, and had the dogs out as much as possible. Barry had taken some amazing photos of them over the summer months and in doing so, we'd given up on hiding the e-collars.

That summer I'd started posting on Instagram about Jace's reality; the challenges we'd faced for years, his history, and how we were progressing. Followers were shocked at how deeply Jace's issues went but for me it was freeing.

At the same time it allowed others who were struggling with their dogs to see they weren't the only ones. What followed were multiple Xolo owners reaching out to me for direction. I loved sharing *Jace's Journey* with others and building relationships within the Xoloitzcuintli community; it made me feel I wasn't alone.

Of course by this point I was ready to go to the mats with anyone who wanted to question my dedication to my dogs, or call me cruel for using tools they might not understand, or in some cases, condemn.

I was living his journey, they weren't. Jace was the obvious transformation, but Xoco was benefitting from these tools too.

Unexpectedly, no one said a thing.

Sure, there had been questions about the e-collar from curious bystanders along the way who stopped to admire and ask about Xoco, but they were without avarice.

On the other hand I wasn't eager to show the prongs.

Prongs stir up vitriol in people—and I get it, they look punishing, but I wasn't prepared to deal with hatred spewing in my direction from people who would rather see my dog suffer from debilitating fears, terrified of his shadow, rather than live a long life being able to navigate the world.

That sort of mentality was not something I could wrap my head around.

All that time, while working with Jace, I was out training Xoco as well.

Just like with Jace, we did fun rapid-fire drills indoors and I had been persistent in working on her off-leash recall outdoors.

She was quite amazing, and continued to improve on all fronts, except on her leash heel.

I'd let that slide because I was focused on Jace, and on longer walks Barry was the one who handled her. He was much less consistent and she would happily drag him all over the place when he held her leash.

We transitioned her to a training collar with rubber tips, like Jace's, and saw immediate improvement.

Again, the communication was there: pull = immediate pressure; stop pulling = pressure released. Along with that were quick turns and circle eights to ensure she was paying attention to her handler on walks. I knew just throwing a tool at a dog, e-collar, prong or whatever, did not fix a problem. I needed to dedicate more time to the process.

But honestly, with the prong it took so little pressure to have her by my side; she became a joy to walk.

In the spring I had purchased a canister of dog and coyote repellent. Pepper spray is not legal in Canada but in this form it was. I wore it attached to a carabineer on my Hurtta trainer's vest—a multi-pocketed water-repellent vest with built in: poop dispenser, cell phone pocket, and treat pocket with removable washable liner. The vest had become invaluable and one of the best things I'd ever invested in. I could just throw it on and had everything I needed. The back hammock pouch was perfect for gloves, secondary leashes, or toys.

Early on the morning of September 8th I was walking past Fisherman's Wharf near Granville Island with Jace. The wharf was always locked up overnight, and as I passed the gate, a man was climbing over it toward us. We locked eyes briefly but I kept walking. It was still slightly dark, and that section of the seawall had no street lighting.

I had a bad feeling.

I grabbed my pepper spray and continued walking eastward with it in my hand—simultaneously I trying to remove the clear tape I'd placed over the nozzle (for safety) with my teeth.

Jace stopped to pee and I took the opportunity to check my six.

Sure enough, the man was following us, he was mumbling something, but all I heard clearly was *dog*. But then he turned around and went back toward the wharf. Proceeding, I continued to monitor him and saw he had a bike leaning against the fence he'd been scaling and was now riding toward us, but then I lost track of him as I took a curve on the pathway.

A female runner passed, then about 20 meters farther a couple also passed us, also heading westward toward the man on the bike I could no longer see.

I relaxed somewhat and kept walking, crossing the single road access onto Granville Island to a grassy spot where Jace finally decided to poop. As he was doing so, the man appeared again slowing as he passed us. Again he mumbled something incoherent, but again I heard the word *dog*. He angled his bike back toward us and I yelled out, "Back away!"

Instead he circled us. As he was doing so I repeated, "Back away!"

I was then holding the canister in front of my body arm outstretched.

He ignored me and circled again, closer this time. I warned him once more and putting Jace behind me, let loose with the spray, right into his face. While he stumbled off into some bushes, I hoofed it out of there and flagged a female passerby to call 911.

Nothing ever came of it; it was a low priority threat, as no one was hurt.

I learned a few of things that morning; primarily no one was ever getting at my dogs—I would go down fighting—also never to tape the canister nozzle or go out without my phone again.

I ended up buying a body camera.

The DNA test we'd submitted from Jace came back from Embark Veterinary in early September. As expected he was 100-percent Xoloitzcuintli. What was a bit of a revelation—his coefficient of inbreeding (COI)—was extremely low at two-percent. My fear was the backyard breeders he came from had been inbreeding, which was common in the worst of them. It did not prove Jace's extreme fears were not the result of breeding, but for me it was evidence that his lack of exposure and socialization as a puppy were the most likely causes of his fragile mental health.

However, while his health results came back exceptional, his alanine amionotransferase activity (ALT) was low normal. That genotype was an indicator of liver health and Jace's was lower than average, therefore we needed to keep an eye on it, as an increase in ALT could be evidence of liver damage. Getting him off all the meds seemed more imperative to me than ever.

Xoco's results came back clean of all 209 genetic health conditions tested and her COI was an equally low three-percent.

Something I had never considered—I honestly didn't know it was a thing—was pet first aid.

Earlier in the summer I'd heard about local pet first aid courses and immediately signed up for an in-person class.

On Sunday September 26th I spent an exhausting, but essential full day learning about pet disease prevention and early disease detection as well as everything from how stop bleeding, set broken bones, dealing with puncture wounds and snake bites to cardio pulmonary respiration (CPR) and artificial respiration (AR).

It was invaluable, even though I prayed I'd never have to use it.

Around this time I'd started implementing more structure in the dogs' everyday indoor life.

Thanks to consistency, I was seeing amazing progression outside, which meant it was finally sinking into my thick skull I needed continuity inside too.

The structure looked like this: each morning upon waking I would take Jace for a walk first. Xoco would immediately go to *place* (closed crate) while I took him out for the first half hour.

Upon return, Jace would go to *place* (closed crate) and I would take Xoco out for the next half hour.

Once the morning walks were complete, both settled in *place* (open crate) until I released them for breakfast using one of the commands: *come* or *break*.

If they had their e-collars on I would often use tone to call them, as I did outdoors.

After breakfast they immediately returned to *place* (open crate) and remained there until I took them out for a pee, or a walk.

Each time the dogs came back inside after a walk, they knew immediately to go to their *place* until released. Pre-meals, they went to *place*. Post meals they went to *place*.

Even if I released them almost immediately—for example after a meal—I was building expectation and consistency in their daily routine. Routine is important for all dogs, even more so for anxious dogs like Jace.

In the case of visitors, *place* was essential.

I learned not to release them from *place* until they settled and were calm enough to come out and greet guests politely; that was sometimes 15 minutes but could easily stretch to an hour. Xoco's enthusiastic affection when greeting with guests was something I prepared people for; Jace would hang back and hope visitors would notice him—when they did he quickly became their best friend.

Consistency was paying off.

I wish I had started, had trusted in the indoor structure advice from the beginning of my introduction to balanced training. I was late to the party but I was finally there.

Month 48: Pen to Paper

THRICE DAILY WALKS CONTINUED boosting Jace's confidence. Not that he was out there looking like he owned the streets, but he was coping much better.

I'd been running six days a week for almost two decades, and while my distance had decreased dramatically in the last couple of years I was still devoted to it.

Xoco had turned 18 months in September, which meant her joints had settled enough to go for runs with me, which she did. The prospect of running with my dog was something I'd always hoped for, but it was obvious in the early days with Jace that wasn't in the cards.

Yet on October 6th I decided to take him with me instead of her.

He was already walking a similar route with me in our hood, for the most part. The run would duplicate our walks, it would just be a longer, and at a slightly faster pace.

Once we hit the seawall I said, "Let's go," and started running.

He trotted after me, looking over his shoulder as if to say, "What are we running from?"

It made me giggle.

We did a mere four kilometres that day, and I tripped over him and went down hard on the concrete bloodying my knee, but I was so elated!

When we returned home, he was relieved but equally proud of himself. I swear he had a little swagger in him.

When I told Barry he was equally surprised and proud of us.

Barry continued to be my biggest fan in all of Jace's rehabilitation. How far Jace had come, how hard I'd worked with him; I'd taken a dog that had to be carried outside to pee a year prior, on a run—past people and bikes and other dogs.

By mid-October Jace was in a perfect heel. It just sort of happened, something finally clicked. Again consistency was paying off.

For the most part I had him on a completely loose leash—the leash swinging from my hip belt. If we were in a busy area, or on a tight sidewalk and I wanted him a little closer I could easily weave the leash between my fingers.

His trust in me was evident and I was honoured by it.

October was also the month Barry finally convinced me to write *Jace's Journey*. He'd watched our boy's progression and was in awe of what I'd accomplished. He knew there were other people out there struggling, and maybe my story, our story, could help.

Before I started the book I knew I had to dig into Jace's past a bit more.

For several years I had been in touch with Sandy, the woman in Cabo San Lucas, Mexico that had rescued Jace and given him a home in her shelter for several months in 2017. Jace and his three littermates—by the way, the only other male in Jace's litter also ended up in Vancouver—were very close to her heart, and the only Xolos she'd ever had in her shelter. I reached out to her on October 27th trying to get a better handle on his beginnings.

She explained to me how a shelter in La Paz had reached out to her for help after rescuing a group of dogs from one home, but they didn't have enough space for them all in the La Paz shelter. Apparently Jace and his littermates were in a yard with several other dogs being bred, and they received no human attention.

Sandy agreed to assist and explained how she and a friend made the two-hour drive to La Paz in a tiny car; they didn't realize how big the Xolo puppies were. On the way back to Cabo, Sandy had two in her lap and she said they craved affection so badly, even once they were in her shelter.

I'd already surmised that of the four, Jace was kept back from adoption the longest because he desperately needed more time. Sandy had brought in a trainer who knew about Xolos to consult on him, but I doubt it helped much. All I knew from Sandy was that trainer had said Jace was incredibly intelligent.

Through no fault of theirs, Jace was already damaged, I'm sure they just hoped he would end up in the right home.

Thankfully he did.

Month 49: Plugging Along

NOVEMBER WAS A QUIET month, we plugged along, doing what we normally did.

The cold weather meant walks needed more preparation in the form of clothing layers for us all.

The calm house structure helped significantly. A year ago, all the dressing and handling they needed just to go outside would have Jace panting and whining, his anxiety building; he was so much better now.

Perfection was a myth. There were good days and bad. Just because he hadn't been whining often didn't mean it didn't happen. Some days he was just more anxious than others—no rhyme, no reason.

Car rides were still a challenge.

Let me clarify: car rides to the beach were a challenge.

To stop the whining I was recommended to: put him in a *down* in the backseat and use the e-collar transmitter to correct his behaviour, and not let him out of the car at the beach until he calmed down.

Putting him in a *down* was the safest in my opinion. Meaning, if he saw another dog outside the car near him there was a possibility of a reaction. While that sort of barrier reaction to other visible dogs had almost disappeared, occasionally it would happen if a dog were too close.

I did not want him to redirect onto Xoco.

A fearful dog does not think clearly and can lash out and just start biting at anything in its path.

Even in a *double down*—body down and head down—he would make a high-pitched whistling-whine.

So I tried letting him sit up, but correcting him with the e-collar slowly increasing the stim level; it just seemed to amp him up.

Honestly, as the main driver and trainer in our home, I didn't feel safe managing him while steering and shifting.

Once at the beach, I knew both dogs needed to immediately poop, and we always wanted to beat other dog owners to the off-leash beach so we might be lucky enough to have some off-leash time. Ergo holding them in the car for too long wasn't something I wanted to do.

Months later I was still deciding the best way to deal with the pre-beach drama he was dishing out. He was most certainly being a brat about it; I knew this because it never happened on the way home, nor did he whine when I was the sole human occupant in the car.

Nonetheless, *down* was winning out. The grumble whining was a fraction of what it used to be, so I was leaning on a theory, which was: as Jace became less anxious over time, so would his drama. And in fact by February Jace had started putting himself into a *double down* as soon as he grew anxious without our command; it helped, but his bratty whistling often continued.

November was also the first time in two years Jace had been for a check-up and his vaccinations. With vet clinics closed to owners thanks to COVID there was no way, barring an emergency, I was going to let Jace go in alone.

Much to my relief, we were able to go in together—and in he did, with no hesitation at all, and no use of the e-collar tone needed.

On all previous visits, Jace would need to be carried in between Barry and myself; vet equalled meltdown.

Of course he was still anxious, but I was just seeing so many changes in him— some tiny, some obvious.

After a typical check-up and catching up on his vaccinations, the vet and I spoke about Jace's meds. Clonidine was the next to go, he would be completely weaned off by December. However my vet was wary of taking him off the final one, the Fluoxetine (aka Prozac). Her own dog was back on it after she tried to wean it off, so she felt it was best Jace remain on it based on her own dog's experience.

I was at a point in training where I felt I really, really wanted him off the meds.

I was equating him being on medication with my own lack of success in training, as if I wasn't enough, or doing as much as I should.

Additionally, my concern over how these meds could affect Jace's long-term health was troubling, but I was equally aware that taking him off completely could mean if we ever needed them again, there was a good chance they wouldn't work the next time.

Together we decided to give it six months, until the next June, and reconsider at that time.

Over the past year my engagement with the Xolo community had increased dramatically, as did questions about my training process. I began having long conversations with other struggling dog owners—primarily of Xolos—looking for direction.

I was honoured but cautious, I'd always prefer someone talk to a professional trainer, but I felt if I were able to lend him or her some insight into my own experience, they might be able to form a better opinion regarding their own options.

Because I knew from experience, not all trainers were open-minded.

I followed many trainers on Instagram, both balanced and R+ and I was vaguely aware of the social media battles going on. I didn't want any part of that drama but in the end folks were pigeonholed; you're either on their side or you were against them.

I had been placed firmly into the "tool user" category, which left me open to vitriol and attacks from the force free community. I was told outright it didn't matter what my story, or Jace's was, I was wrong and a horrible human being.

Quickly concluding there here was no use arguing with those folks, I simply blocked them.

What the anti-tool population didn't understand was I had nothing against force free training, if it worked. For canines like Jace, I'd seen proof it didn't work. There were dogs all around the world like Jace; or they were possibly human or dog aggressive—R+ just wasn't enough for so many them.

In public I saw the looks from people who caught glimpses of the prong collars on my dogs, no one to date had said a word to me, but I had a lot of confidence by that point and walked tall with a strong stride. That sort of poise not only translated to Jace, but to anyone who might think to offer unsolicited opinions.

Month 50: Little Things

FOR OWNERS OF EASY dogs, some of the tiny developments in Jace's newfound poise likely wouldn't have been noticeable.

To us they were part of a bigger picture. Brick by brick we were building fortitude.

For example, Jace would never crawl under things that might touch his back. Suddenly he was scooting under Barry's legs as he rested them on the coffee table. He was also asking for more affection, even pushing his much bossier little sister aside to make room for himself. In the past he would stand back and wait for me to come to him.

Putting a harness or a heavier coat on didn't faze him nearly the way it used to—he wasn't crumpling anymore. Squeezing his body between a barely open door and its frame was a new trick we'd never seen.

Jace's slouch was a little less obvious.

He's always had a bit of a swayback and when in a fearful situation he would make himself smaller, tail tucked, haunches lower to the ground…

We were seeing his body language change.

From an Instagram follower, I found out about a pack walk group in East Vancouver.

Knowing reactivity was our next big hurdle, I signed up for two weeks in a row.

The environment in East Vancouver, specifically the busy intersections we crossed were far bigger triggers for Jace than other dogs were.

He was so environmentally aware and exceedingly nervous; proximity to other dogs had zero impact on him. He was flooded by his surroundings and was unable to focus on one single stressor.

Granted I didn't get close to any of them because they weren't neutral dogs either, nor were they being walked with the structure I found so important with Jace. Even with the pack walk leaders being trainers; I didn't completely trust the situation.

I'd come too far to compromise Jace's trust in an uncontrolled encounter.

But hallelujah, near the end of December I stumbled across a balanced trainer working in Vancouver!

Ironically, a sponsored advertisement on Instagram led me to her.

The ad was for some waterproof sneakers Barry and I planned on ordering for us; the person in the sponsored video was a dog trainer named Kelly.

I checked out Kelly's account and her website The Pack Dog Training, then immediately filled out an online form and booked a consultation with her for the earliest possible date in the New Year.

While I later found out she considered herself more of a LIMA trainer, with a strong open-minded approach, everything Kelly stood for seemed to resonate; primarily she had a likeminded approach to my use of training tools. I also felt advanced enough in my skills I'd immediately know if she was the right fit.

At that point—and going forward—I needed someone with a fresh set of eyes, someone I could bounce ideas off of; a person that could assist in our progression.

> When looking for a trainer, do your research. Trust your instincts. Check their social media posts—can you clearly see they have a proven track record helping owners, and dogs like yours.

JACE'S JOURNEY

Practicing down-stay on a pack walk in East Van

PART 9
Month 51: Bitchy Dog Mom

THE ONGOING BARRAGE OF off-leash dogs weighed heavily on me.

It was winter and the *Leash Your Fu*king Dog* hoodie and t-shirt I'd been sporting summer and fall while walking the dogs, weren't visible under my winter coats.

I was increasingly more vocal.

I didn't go looking for conflict, but it found me.

I'd had confrontations with a number of locals on our morning walks.

On the plus side, once I lost my cool with someone, they tended to avoid me in the future, or at least leash their dog when they saw me with mine.

I was exhausted with people thinking they were above the law, that their dogs were special in some way. If I were with Jace, I would avoid conflict or raised voices unless we were cornered.

However, with Xoco being confident, I could call people out and she would remain relatively chill.

I began to realize people didn't know I had two dogs because they look so much alike, and I walked them separately.

It was then I knew I couldn't give off-leash dog owners a pass if I was with Xoco, and then lose it if I were with Jace. I needed to be consistent and advocate for him, even if he wasn't with me.

If people saw me ignoring their poor behaviour with one dog, they would assume they could do it again; the next time I could very well be with Jace.

Simultaneously, I knew I had to work harder on Xoco's off-leash behaviour as a responsible owner.

When we were in the local off-leash park—as we were a couple times per week—I trained her to go into a *down* and *stay* as on-leash dogs walked by, or when a new dog came into the park.

There were two reasons for this.

Firstly, it was unfair of her to approach an on-leash dog that just happened to be walking by when she was off-leash.

Secondly, I didn't let her play with dogs I didn't know. Getting her into a *down* allowed me to quickly analyze the situation and either hold her in that position or leash her if I wasn't certain.

Over the next month she got better at this until she was putting herself into a *down* as soon as she saw another dog. Did she sometimes break her *down*? Sure.

If the dog got too close, or was a playmate, she would totally break it.

But it was much better than the alternative—my dog running amok and possibly scaring another dog, or triggering an unknown canine being walked by an unaware owner.

If I could help it, it wasn't going to happen on my watch.

My mantra became; trust no dogs, trust no owners—unless I knew them.

> Make your dog your priority. Don't concern yourself with other dogs unless you need to. That means managing your dog's behaviour, for the wellbeing of everyone around you.

Little by little I was pushing Jace out of his comfort zone. Something I hadn't done in a while was walk him in a different direction, on a new street and for longer periods mid-day. I started with a couple blocks along new streets very close to home, and then extended those walks. Sometimes I veered on to a very busy street for brief periods before bringing him back to a quieter side street. I would often alternate our direction to places he had never been.

Some days our walks got longer and sometimes in more chaotic environments; on others the route was more relaxing and quieter.

I could see his coping mechanisms improving little by little.

Month 52: Sinking or Swimming

JACE'S BIRTHDAY HAD ARBITRARILY been set on February 1st. I'm not sure why, because based on his rescue timeline and adoption, he was likely born closer to January 1st.

Even so, we celebrated each year with a cake from a local dog bakery. That year I decided to make it myself. It was sloppy but fun to do, and Jace loved it.

What I didn't love was he was now five years old and I was beginning to struggle with the reality of him ageing.

I felt his mortality more deeply than my own and I wanted to slow down time.

On a much happier note, in recent weeks I'd noticed Jace paying me more attention when we were walking.

He'd never been focused on me enough to reward and treat; he was always too suspicious of his environment.

I didn't force it. I just walked with him quietly, him doing his job, staying at my side in a heel and me doing mine, watching out for him while keeping my eyes peeled for possible triggers.

Weekend walks at Spanish Banks was where it started. When we were off the main path and walking along the sandy shore, the only sounds were the waves and the seagulls. It was peaceful.

One morning I caught his attention by clicking my tongue—when he looked to me, I said "good" and gave him a treat. He was more easily motivated because I never feed breakfast until post morning walks.

That new eye contact and treat acceptance bled over into weekday morning walks around Granville Island. Sometimes he'd engage with me for 30 meters, sometimes half of our 30-minute walk. One morning, while juggling a path between two off-leash, and one on-leash dog, he maintained eye contact with me almost the entire time.

I was thrilled.

By the end of the month, from one end of Spanish Banks to the other—nearly two kilometres—his attention was on me for the entire walk. He ate me out of treats. The trend was our friend.

Around this time I was spending more time chatting with a fellow Xolo owner living in Mexico City. Of her three, only the youngest, an intermediate male, came from a good breeder. Her older standard male, the result of inbreeding, had a lot of issues similar to Jace's, so we had much in common. While we handled their unique environmentally suspicious natures differently, it was cathartic to speak with someone who understood my challenges.

She and I agreed that until you have a dog with so much awareness and so many triggers, you truly didn't notice the world around you the same way we did.

A screaming child, a car backfiring, a revving engine, a skateboard, the clangs of a truck full of tools hitting a pothole, or a group of teens speaking at high volumes, were all terrifying to Jace. I had personally become extremely sensitive to those sounds, and I felt his discomfort. Each commotion was like a shot to the solar plexus, which I desperately tried not to show in my demeanour, for his sake.

Back in January I had signed the dogs up for a one-on-one swim lesson at a local dog pool.

Xolos are not swimming dogs.

They don't have the body shape for it, despite their webbed paws. I'd heard of few who could, or would, swim. Plus their lack of a coat didn't help, they get cold easily, and fur provides some buoyancy.

However, I was all about new experiences for them. For Jace it was confidence building, and for Xoco, well I thought if any Xolo would swim, it would be her. Summer days at the beach she was always in the water, playfully charging forward—but never deeper than her upper chest.

My concern, although she was never far from us, was her hitting a dip in the ocean floor and losing her ability to touch. I wanted to know, if only for a few seconds, she could paddle enough to get her feet under her again.

Having the pool to ourselves seemed like fun, even with the yapping and barking of the dogs in the attached day-care echoing around us and piercing any calm.

On February 6th we entered the pool. As expected Jace was agitated, not unlike when I took him to nose work classes the year prior. However, Barry had never seen Jace like that and it made him anxious too. I stayed up near the pool with two bags of chopped beef hotdogs, while the wetsuit-clad instructor lured them down ramps into the water.

Jace was engaged within minutes, he was far braver than I expected, and was actually going to her when she called him. I knew he'd never go in, but that wasn't the point.

Xoco was more enthusiastic, but also far too canny to descend the wooden ramps deeper than her knees, so we put a harness on her.

About 35-minutes into the session, the instructor was twice able to grasp the harness and pull Xoco in, holding her while she paddled.

Even the instructor admitted Xoco wasn't going to be a swimmer, which didn't deter me. I still wanted her to know how to paddle if need be.

I signed up for one more class in March.

Pushing boundaries a little more with longer walks in new directions

PART 10

Month 52: Evolution

WITH MY CONFIDENCE IN training Jace building I was starting to come to some personal conclusions regarding his needs. I was able to cherry pick techniques to test his responses, and loosen up on some of his structure.

Any good trainer knows there is no one-size-fits-all when it comes to training dogs, and as his human I was more aware of that than many.

Meaning I was leaning more toward giving Jace reassurance when I felt he needed it, just a gentle touch, not coddling. He had always loved leaning into me and I'd been noticing when he was highly anxious on a walk he would lean into me so closely I would almost trip.

To me that was a clear sign that even during moments of intense stress he sought some comfort.

While it didn't make an immediate difference, over the next month I could see him relaxing minutely in unexpected places.

I started seeking more guidance from a number of sources, not just Xolo owners, not just pros, but from humans like myself, novices struggling with their own dogs. Some were first time owners forced into training a challenging dog; some had a wider range of experience. Others were trainers with multi-pronged approaches; they relied heavily on R+ but were not against using tools in certain situations.

Being someone who had always struggled with just doing what was told to me, I wanted to keep my options open. I'd trained Jace on my own, slowly, because I needed to see his reactions to my coaching, and I wanted to make up my own mind about the very techniques I had been implementing. My desire to examine all alternatives was growing.

Jace was a special case, I'd gotten him this far, I could get him further, but there would always be limitations.

Exposing him gently to scary things in his world was imperative, but how far did I push? He truly only needed to exist within a limited area: home, the beach, and our neighbourhood... Yet I felt if I exposed him to triggers outside his little world, it might make his bubble seem even safer, make him more confident.

As always those questions kept me awake at night.

I wanted Barry to be part of it, so our initial assessment with Kelly occurred on Sunday February 13th. In hindsight, a Sunday around the highly touristic Granville Island was a huge mistake; it was sunny and ergo horribly busy—pre-pandemic busy.

By the time we found each other, Jace was totally flooded. Cars, people and dogs surrounded us. We had an initial introduction and about 15 minutes of the discussion was based on Jace's type of reactivity, I'd sent Kelly an entire novella on his history—as well as the video of Jace and I walking I'd sent to Josh the summer before—so she was somewhat prepared to see his fear.

Still, I don't think even she was expecting his level of anxiety—no one ever did.

Getting right to it, Kelly brought out one of her larger dogs, a brawny pit bull aptly named Ferdinand. We were standing about five meters from her van when Ferdinand jumped down from it, Jace immediately reacted—hell, so did I when I saw him—but it was brief.

Kelly and Ferdinand followed us toward our home lane. Once back in his own territory, Jace reacted again.

Following Ferdinand, we walked back and forth down our lane with two more of her dogs, one at a time. The second was a larger alpha, a Dogo Argentino, and the third a playful Pit Bull, Border Collie and Boxer mix named Cooper. Jace reacted to both. Granted we were on his home turf and I already knew he was territorial.

I did not correct him with his e-collar in any of those situations, just a verbal *no*, when he did react.

Kelly was the trainer I truly felt I needed at that moment in time, so I decided to sign up for a series of pack walks with her. As much as it tortured me—and I struggled mightily—allowing other dogs into Jace's personal space I knew there was no way he would improve his coping mechanisms without Kelly and her pack.

Being as booked as she was, our sessions wouldn't be starting until April but I was used to waiting when it came to Jace's progression.

Over the next week, each time I took Jace for a run he reacted to a dog. It was concerning for me as I'd never had him react to a dog on a run prior to that time. His behaviour was extra troubling for me and I started to question whether I was doing the right thing with these pack walks with Kelly. Jace had built his trust in me—had I let him down in our own lane by letting a dog near enough to him that he felt he had to protect himself.

Had I lost his trust?

An internal battle ensued, but deep down I knew I had to try and work with him through this part of his training. I truly felt this was the last big hurdle we needed to face.

Granted, I knew, Kelly knew, and so did Barry, Jace was never going to be a normal dog. He would never be totally confident, he was damaged too much for that, but having him cope in the world and facing his fears was the objective. It included becoming more neutral around other dogs.

Post pack walk. Photo: Kelly Argue of The Pack Dog Training

Month 53: Saudade

MARCH CAME IN LIKE a lamb.

We celebrated Xoco's second birthday on March 1st and it was warm enough for her to play outside naked. It was the first time either dog had been outside without some form of clothing since October.

I made her a large bone shaped cake and as I pulled it out of the oven to set on a cooling rack I had mini-meltdown. It had been building for months, and it suddenly hit me; I was having an identity crisis.

I looked at that cake, and thought, when did I start making dog cakes?

I was an international wine journalist, I spent a large part of my year with winemakers over multi-course meals, trotting through vineyards all over the world, sampling wines from barrels and writing about it. I had so many stories and memories tied up in my wine career.

I didn't know who I was anymore.

The pandemic had put the kibosh on my international and local travels, I was still writing but the content seemed frivolous compared to what used to pour out of me.

I missed being me, the wine writer.

I was the queen of carry-on, a well-seasoned traveller, wining and dining in exotic locations. After almost two decades of that lifestyle I was a stay-at-home dog mom who baked cakes and spent hour after hour walking them, training them, keeping them healthy and groomed.

I'd never had children; in part because I wanted the freedom I didn't feel children allowed; yet here I was, for all intents and purposes, a mom.

It was bittersweet, it was Saudade: a Portuguese word referring to profound longing, and nostalgia. A perfect description for how I was feeling for my pre-COVID life.

Additionally, I had just turned down my annual trip to Tuscany for the Chianti Classico vintage release, which was scheduled for later that month. That depressed me. I wanted to get back out there and see my comrades from India, the Czech Republic, China, the USA and the EU, and to talk wine rather than reactivity.

The primary reason I turned it down was the dogs. Barry did not have confidence handling Jace. If I accepted that trip, he would feel he needed to take time off work in order to give them even a fraction of the exercise I did per. In part it was my fault for not insisting he take more time with Jace, trading off with me, while I walked Xoco instead. But I also knew it was less about the act of walking and more about his apprehension in handling a reactive Jace.

Agitated, I reached out to a fellow Xolo owner in New York. Mishan and I been friends on social media for several years. Her Xolo, also a rescue, was the same age as Jace. Over the past couple of years we'd become confidants, often sending daily videos with light-hearted banter. Our conversations differed from those of my other Xolo-owning friends in that we primarily spoke about ourselves: our careers, families, the daily slog, food, and our cultural upbringings.

She was quick to lend an ear, which helped pull me out of my funk.

Feeling better I went ahead made that hell out of that cake for Xoco, and it was glorious. Her joy, and that of Jace for his piece of her pink-iced bone cake, lifted my spirits.

I had so much love for them both.

Still, that day was a red flag; I continued to feel as though I was straddling two worlds; I didn't know where I fully belonged.

I knew Barry would be happy if I decided never to travel again, and study dog training as a career path instead. While I seriously considered shadowing trainers I respected, I didn't see it as my new calling. Honestly I felt too old to start again, and I could not dedicate the sheer number of working hours trainers put in.

Time would tell what my post-COVID life would look like.

After speaking quite extensively with Vancouver's Animal Control one afternoon, Barry bought me a GoPro to wear on my walks with the dogs. It was not only for our own safety, but to keep track of the very off-leash dogs we were protesting.

> Consider buying a GoPro or a body camera. They are excellent for safety and reviewing footage of your own reactions in certain situations, highlighting where you can improve.

Animal control seemed just as frustrated as we were, or they were at least sympathetic, but as in all politics, their proverbial hands were tied. They needed constant visual proof of all illegal activity.

I swear, the moment I started wearing that camera, people started leashing their dogs far more frequently.

Over the course of that first month however, I did get some amazing off-leash footage to share on social media. It was also an amazing way for me to keep track of my own reaction to other dogs when in proximity to Jace, as well as my handling of him.

I was far calmer than I realized. My inner turmoil didn't seem to translate to my voice or to leash tightening.

On March 7th I received an email that Kelly had a cancellation the next day if I was available. I grabbed the opportunity.

Since it was a weekday, we agreed on Granville Island again, hoping it would be quieter than our last session.

I met her near the Granville Island Hotel, where we caught up briefly before she brought out her first dog, an elderly Chihuahua she knew would completely ignore Jace.

The surroundings were more chaotic than expected, but manageable. Jace's body language was typical in that sort of mid-day environment; he was tightly-wound, tail tucked under his belly, head swivelling, and just managing to cope.

While I had seen him explode in similar situations after encountering so many triggers, I wanted to see how he would react with such a neutral dog.

He was fully aware of the Chihuahua but ignored it, more concerned about a construction worker a few feet away. I released Jace from his heel and kept a loose leash as the four of us walked around the perimeter of the hotel once.

Kelly then brought Ferdinand out—the same dog Jace reacted too a few weeks back—for a repeat of the same stroll. Along the way, we stopped and watched other people and dogs pass. Kelly encouraged me to breathe, to emanate calm. If I couldn't calm myself, he wouldn't either. I have to admit, I thought I was cool as a cucumber; Kelly could obviously see something I couldn't.

This is what I knew I needed; a fresh set of experienced eyes.

As we kept still watching the world go by, I felt Jace ease very slightly. The repetitiveness of a route he walked each morning with me, and again that very day with Kelly and her dogs, seemed to be working.

Finally Cooper, Kelly's outgoing Pit Bull, Collie and Boxer mix joined us. Jace had also reacted to Cooper on their first meeting, but by the time we got half way around the hotel he was walking right beside Cooper and Kelly.

That was a huge win.

Both exhausted, Jace and I crashed when we got home.

Nearly constant rain plagued us for the next month and a half.

However we did get a couple of great off-leash days on the tidal flats. Jace was in his glory, tail straight in the air, prancing and positive. I realized I used to obsess about getting him out there at every possible opportunity in previous years because it was his main form of exercise. With the longer daily walks since last summer, I didn't get jittery if we missed a low tide.

His reactivity seemed to be lessening as well. I can't be sure if it was the result of walking alongside Cooper and Kelly, or my hard won fight to remain calm as much as possible—perhaps both.

As well, his increased confidence in recent months didn't hurt.

Don't get me wrong; walking with Jace in daylight hours in busy places was still startling to most people. He oozed fear, but it was less apparent than a few months earlier.

March was a turning point in many ways.

I decided to self-publish this book based on everything I had researched and the time it would take to actually get published. I didn't want to sit around another six months just hoping for a publisher's response, and then wait another year to start the whole process.

Our good friends and neighbours Don and Nina also brought a new puppy home in March. Their beloved boy Decker had passed away suddenly from cancer the previous October. They'd been devastated.

Don missed having a dog and convinced Nina to get another Frenchie, which they did. She was four months old. They named her Frieda and she was a tiny darling thing that loved other dogs and people. Xoco, my little miss congeniality, was immediately enamoured.

I was stressed.

Jace's reactivity to Decker from the moment we'd moved in had been exhausting; I didn't want a repeat with Frieda. Decker was fearless and would stand behind Don and Nina's gate watching the world outside with curiosity. If Jace saw, smelled or heard Decker he would start up, barking and detonating like he was going to rip anything in front of him apart to get to the smaller dog.

Frieda was not Decker, she was so much smaller and a different sex, but still I was worried Jace might frighten her.

So I hatched a plan to have them walk in proximity, starting in a neutral nearby park. On the morning of the last Saturday in March Nina, Frieda, Barry, and Xoco walked from our homes together toward the park where Jace and I waited.

When they saw us, I had them turn around and head home. Jace and I followed at a respectful distance; I kept a minimum of three meters back. Frieda was very curious about Jace and tended to turn and stare at him, so I made sure we had space if Jace freaked out.

Jace was aware of her but ignored her with all the other people and activity around us.

We walked home. Nina and Frieda went through their gate, and Barry, Xoco, Jace and I through ours immediately after. We did not stop and chat. I didn't want Jace to fixate on her, but once we were in our separate yards, we did chat over the fence. Jace knew the puppy was next door, but unlike his reactions to Decker, he remained calm.

I was elated.

I was confident Jace would never be Frieda's BFF, but I needed him to respect her and her space: to not be an ass.

We agreed to do it again whenever possible.

Pack Walk. Photo: Kelly Argue of The Pack Dog Training

Month 54: When Pigs Fly

IN EARLY APRIL I sent my manuscript off to an acquaintance in the UK I'd met on Instagram. Brigitta was a dog behaviourist, and owner of Poochology. Her focus was: anxiety, aggression, trauma/PTSD and rescues. She also had a reactive rescue dog of her own. I found her posts extremely helpful—she was highly knowledgeable. I asked her if she would read the book and perhaps write a review, or even a forward.

She said she'd be happy to read it.

Talk about stressful. I'm a writer, I write all the time, but never anything so personal, and not an entire book. I'd edited it a several of times already, but after I sent her the manuscript I went back and edited again. I found plenty of small errors; I knew I'd review it many more times, so I wasn't overly concerned.

It also made me reread—and cry, every, damn, time—Jace's history over the past few years, again and again. The book was written proof of his progression and gave me the opportunity to acknowledge what worked and what didn't.

For us the *double down* was, no-pun-intended, a flop.

For most dogs, putting them in a *down*, then training a second form of *down*, where the head also rests—body down, head down—is an excellent way to instill calm. It's a way of training a dog to be still. The theory is, in a full resting *down*, the brain slows and decreases anxiety.

While I still thought it was an excellent command, for Jace it didn't work.

Even if his head was completely lowered, he was still in high state of anxiety. Forcing it, or trying to, only stressed him more. So I gave up on it.

Just because it didn't work for him doesn't mean it wouldn't for any number of other dogs.

Granted Jace continued putting himself in a *double down* when in the car if he started to really amp up, and that was fine. It was his decision and his way of coping—yet even when he selected to do it himself it didn't fully work.

Jace needed extra time for everything.

Thinking back to how much he used to whine in the car was proof he was improving, albeit gradually.

During our Sunday morning car ride to the beach on the 17th of April, I decided to try a new tactic to encourage serenity. As soon as we got in the car I had Barry start to reward calm behaviour with treats. He continued to treat unless Jace got agitated. If Jace got whiny, the treats would stop.

Xoco, who was always calm, continued to get treats. It took several tries, but Jace finally started to figure it out. He stopped being bratty and he got a treat, he started the unwanted behaviour again, the treats stopped. It was likely the quietest morning trip to the beach ever.

I did not believe it was simply a case of us going about things the wrong way prior to that morning. If we'd attempted this method a year before, it wouldn't have worked. Just rewarding him, positive reinforcement only, would have failed; it had failed time and again, because Jace was in a totally different place a year prior. He was always so stressed he would never have taken food while at that threshold.

More than a year of working on boundaries, correcting unwanted behaviour and building confidence is exactly what got us to that very point; a time where he was able to stop, think, and then accept rewards based on good behaviour.

Like his newfound ability to engage with me while walking—and getting rewarded for it—he was coping better in all situations; he was continuously evolving.

Jace's challenges were complex to say the least; so was his cumulative progression.

To further that last statement I did something else I never considered before.

I'd always had a deep dislike of retractable leashes—even before I had a dog. As a runner they were dangerous. How many times had I almost been clothes-lined when a fluffer darted across the seawall right in front of me, the owner oblivious? Once I had a reactive dog, I disliked them more.

Pigs must have sprouted wings because I bought two.

I decided on the Fida brand retractable with auto braking system, the same five-meter (16-foot) extension versions trainer Kelly used with some of her dogs.

I didn't buy them for use in the city, but for beach walks and possible hikes.

I also purchased two tactical-style body harnesses for the dogs, and ordered some new Velcro patches in preparation for a fast approaching family road trip.

The harness concerned me most. As I'd previously stated, items touching Jace's back were triggers; he would crawl if they touched him the wrong way. I was shocked at how well he responded to having something around him with that sort of structure. With the harness on top of his lightweight jacket, he seemed oblivious to it.

Saturday morning April 9th I took the harness and the retractable for a test run on the first portion of our walk along the Spanish Banks' shore.

At first Jace was a bit confused, he stayed close to my side, the usual span of his short leash. Without him realizing, I slowed down as we walked, allowing him to pull ahead, when he turned around and realized I was several meters behind, he stopped and waited. I repeated the process a couple more times until he understood he had extra freedom

It allowed him to sniff and explore at his own pace, and the results were amazing. This new privilege gave him to chance to be the dog he hadn't been able to before. It calmed him.

As soon as we left the beach and hit the path toward the off-leash beach I put him back into a heel on his short leash, which was attached to the prong and e-collar. The reason was twofold: firstly my vision was obscured on the path and I needed to see what was approaching. Secondly I wanted to put that structure back in place before allowing him his next freedom, being off-leash mid-walk at the beach.

For me it was about being able to control the situation if I couldn't control the environment.

Remember, Jace on a quiet beach was a very different dog than Jace walking around our neighbourhood where he was much more burdened by the world. In those cases, when stressed, he fared better in a tight heel.

The following morning he did so well, was so chill overall, I allowed that loose heel to continue for almost the entirety of the walk—though I did switch out his retractable for a shorter lead. Even so, Jace continued to stop and sniff and just be a dog while trotting along the very path he wouldn't even consider walking eight months before.

What I'm trying to convey was this: his new freedoms were the direct results of all the structure and repetition we'd embraced in recent months. He wouldn't have had those liberties months before because he was too afraid to take advantage of them. He didn't know how to be a dog.

> Train structure to inspire confidence and freedom.

Additionally Jace's routine, especially his usual morning walk, was something I stopped messing with. If I needed to push him a little, I could do so on other walks—and it didn't have to be every day. Although he was coping in new environments, it was still highly stressful for him. Our morning walks needed to be his safety. I stayed the course and didn't mess with the route or the timing much. It was the least I could do.

Another win, we felt we'd finally found a way to prevent Jace's constant ear issues.

We'd gone at least two months since I last had to bandage split ear tips.

In part, he was less stressed overall, and tended to flap/shake less, but we'd devised a simple routine. Since his ears tended to be most vulnerable in the early morning when he first woke and his ears were cold, Barry would put a snood on him when he left for work. That simple step warmed up his ears nicely by the time the rest of us rose. Those first few shake and flaps in the morning after stretching kept his warm ears under wraps. Then just prior to first walk, I would remove the snood and lubricate the tips with an emollient stick meant for paws and noses. It was working brilliantly so far.

Touch wood.

I was also weaning Xoco off her prong collar.

I'd been working on more engagement with her via eye contact when walking, she was being hand fed a good portion of her daily food via treats at that point; I adjusted her twice-daily raw meals accordingly, and it was working admirably.

Like Jace, she required far less correction in terms of leash pressure, or e-collar taps. I truly believed that combination of positive reinforcement and correction was the game changer for both; the process just looked a little different for Xoco than for Jace.

Ironically I'd become very proficient with the use of the e-collar transmitter over the last six months, yet I rarely needed to use the skill. I certainly wasn't complaining though—it meant we were all victorious.

We did two more short pack walks with little Frieda in April. The first was an exact repeat of the first one in March, but Jace and she were much closer in proximity. The second time I had them walk around our block. Nina, Frieda, Barry, and Xoco walked out into the lane first. Jace and I followed.

We crossed paths with no fewer than six dogs on that walk, it was a stressful one for him with so much going on, but he didn't react to anything. Again he was aware of her, that she was living next door, but he ignored her.

The following Monday morning, as we returned from our morning walk, Don was outside our gates with Frieda, I stopped to chat with him, keeping a respectable distance, and Jace paid her no attention. I was still not going to push it, but during all four of their encounters, Jace had been a champ.

Slow and steady.

On April 19th we had our second official pack walk with Kelly.

I decided to change the location to a much quieter spot; I wanted to see if Jace's reaction to other dogs would be more pronounced if he had less environmental stimuli around and was able to focus more on her dogs around him.

We met at Vanier Park west of our home.

He was in his usual state of arousal but once again ignored her dogs for the most part, except for a rascal of a Jack Russell Terrier that got in Jace's face. Jace gave him a strong but brief correction. Of the five dogs Jace walked with that day, that was his only reaction. One of Kelly's other clients happened by with his dog and ended up joining in our little pack briefly, Jace was wary of this new dog's energy but it was great to see another dog just happen along and join us for a brief time.

The following week, our Tuesday session was called due to rain and hail. The spring had been almost non-existent so far and everyone was tired of the endless cold and wet days.

We rescheduled for Thursday and Kelly suggested we do walks in threes—Jace and two of hers at a time. For the most part Jace continued blatantly ignoring the other dogs in the pack while getting quite close to a couple. However when Cooper—the dog Jace seemed to be most comfortable with— turned to look at Jace on our last walk of the session, Jace reacted.

It was an almost perfect set up and I had it all recorded on my GoPro.

It went like this. Jace decided to trot up alongside Cooper's right flank, but just as Jace's head was parallel with Cooper's shoulder, Cooper turned quickly—they almost bumped noses, and of course eye contact occurred.

I played the video back in slow motion many times and you could see the instant Jace flipped out. Cooper backed off immediately, I pulled back on Jace's leash and it was over.

Everyone shook it off and we ended the walk on a high note.

While Jace was still snapping at other dogs, it's important to note his reactions were becoming far less frequent and less dramatic, and his recovery time was swift. All the exposure over the past year and the sessions with Kelly were gradually helping.

At the very end of April I switched Jace back to a slip lead.

The metal clip on his biothane lead and prong collar were creating ear issues again. When he shook and his ears flapped, the right one would hit the metal hardware and his ear was in terrible shape again. Where I had struggled with the slip lead initially—it didn't give me near the ability to use light pressure as the prong—he now understood heel, so it worked incredibly well.

The feel of the slip lead's fabric my hands, ease of use and its lighter weight were all pleasing to me. I planned to continue using it going forward, unless he started to backslide, at which point I could go back to the prong.

Pack Walk. Photo: Kelly Argue of The Pack Dog Training

The author and Jace. Photo: Kelly Argue of The Pack Dog Training

PART 11

Month 55: Family Vacation

FOR THE FIRST TIME in five years, since the summer before we got Jace, Barry and I were going away together. There was no one we trusted with the dogs—no one nearby. I knew if Jess, south of us in Washington Sate, was closer I'd trust her with them, but I would never impose as Iorveth was her priority and she would struggle with housing dogs he was not familiar with—fairly so.

In reality, I wanted to take them with us.

If it were a year prior I couldn't see it happening with Jace, not where he was mentally. But I felt he had come so far, was capable of so much more. So, I had convinced a hesitant Barry in January to book a getaway on Vancouver Island.

I told him I felt we were underestimating Jace, and really wanted to see if we could start travelling again, which I was sure was only going to happen as a family unit.

Additionally it was our 25th wedding anniversary in early May and we needed to celebrate somehow.

The plan was to rent an SUV and stay at a resort we knew well. A place on Cox Bay in Tofino we had stayed at several times before. The difference, we used to fly over in a small aircraft each spring for several days. This time we would drive. It would be about a five-hour journey, including what I assumed would be a highly stressful ferry ride.

Planning a five-day getaway with two dogs was no minor undertaking. We weren't even sure if their crates would fold down and fit in the vehicle.

On the morning of May 4th Barry and I went to pick up the rental SUV so we could prepare for a very early morning departure on May 5th.

As it turned out we were able to upgrade to a much larger vehicle that seated six. Which meant my concern over breaking down the crates and taking them with us was immediately alleviated.

At dawn the next morning we went for a quick walk with the dogs then gave them breakfast. In Jace's bowl I placed one-half of an Alprazolam tablet. I had no idea how he was going to travel and wanted to give him a mild sedative to help him deal with what was about to happen; the goal was to expand Jace's bubble not scare him.

Meanwhile Barry packed up all the gear, filling the vehicle with crates and bedding, blankets, clothing, food bowls, treats, toys, collars, leashes, chew sticks, and five days worth of frozen raw food in a cooler. For us, we each had a small bag of clothing, wine and some basic provisions.

It was comical how much stuff we needed to make sure they were completely at home and comfortable. Jace especially.

> Taking a vacation with your dog? Take all their stuff with you to make them comfortable.

Getting into the back seats of the SUV was a bit of a test; the dogs had never jumped up into a car so high, especially as we'd stacked blankets and their beds on top of the seats to keep them cozy for the long drive.

Initially Jace exhibited some wary sort of confusion and light whining.

Once he calmed a bit, Barry made sure to keep the treats coming as I steered the rental toward the Horseshoe Bay ferry terminal.

I had reserved a spot on the ferry to be sure we were stationed on the upper deck where people were allowed to stay in their vehicles, and ergo with their dogs. The first hour, parked and immobile while waiting to board was a bit tense. People and dogs passing the car alerted Jace, but he didn't have a reaction.

Me leaving the vehicle for a bathroom break was the bigger stressor for both; they were far more confident with the entire family unit being together. The 90-minute ferry ride began with a lot of vigilance on their part. Cars were packed in like sardines and the proximity to people as well as strange clanging noises ferry noises kept them alert.

Still, they both engaged and Jace gnawed on his chew stick, which thrilled me. If he was comfortable enough to do that, and take treats, he was in a good place.

An hour and a half after our wheels hit the ground in Nanaimo we stopped for a much-needed pee break and short hike through the muddy rainforest at Cathedral Grove. Two hours later we'd arrived to our new home-away-from-home at the dog-friendly beach resort in Tofino.

I let the dogs wander around the ground-floor suite getting their bearings and sniffing while Barry unloaded our gear and put the crates together.

By the time they had their dinner just after five pm that evening, both dogs seemed completely at ease.

I was floored.

I expected Jace to pace and shake and be his usual stressed self, but he wasn't. He didn't like other guests and dogs walking past our window, but I used low-level stim on the e-collar to correct them both when needed.

I am absolutely certain having all their possessions: bedding and blankets—I didn't wash any prior to the trip because I wanted everything to smell like home— toys, and us, were the most important factors in a successful assimilation.

Waking at dawn on Friday morning we put on all our rain gear and hit the Cox Bay shore just steps from our door. Seeing the beach empty we let them walk and play off-leash for most of the one-point-five kilometres to the south end of the beach and back. Jace was in his glory, tail up, running, and frolicking with his sister.

Honestly I was awestruck at how resilient he was, how content he was with this change of scenery, away from his one true comfort: home.

Back in April, I had hired a local photographer to take photos of the four of us while in Tofino. Being our silver anniversary was a big part of the decision, but I also wanted pictures of the dogs with

Barry in them. He was always behind the lens—I wanted him to be in front of it with us for once.

I'd explained to the photographer we had a fearful dog and wanted to be in an area where there would be less human and canine traffic. He suggested a place near Frank Island during low tide. After lunch we hopped in the car and drove to meet him.

I was concerned a stranger with a camera following us around would spook Jace, but he was far too interested in the few people in the distance and the wind blowing across the expanse of beach. An hour later, much to Jace's relief, we wrapped it up and headed back to the resort. I was looking forward to seeing the images in a couple weeks, but hoped he was able to get a few good shots of Jace, whose tail was tucked during most of the session.

I'd hoped to use one for the cover of this book, which I did.

Our time in Tofino became routine; long morning walks off-leash on the shore, and then chilling indoors for the remainder of the day.

On the second day Jace asked to go out, twice.

He never asked to go out, even at home. He'd rather stay inside where it was safe. I postulated if his ability to see outside clearly had a bearing on him wanting to explore. Did he feel safer, more in control, when he could see his environment and open expanse of the shore through the large front windows before he went out to explore?

Barry would take off with his camera for a while to get some action shots of surfers out in the bay, or pick up food from a local burger and fish shack while I stayed with the dogs.

We decided we would not leave them alone on the trip even though we had the crates. I wasn't sure they were ready for that.

We kept life simple and consistent. Like at home, before meals they would be on *place* in crate, and again after—even if it those times were brief.

I fed them in their own bowls, a very similar meal to what they would have at home, and at the same times of the day.

Both were getting less aroused by traffic walking past our windows—humans and dogs. Jace's reaction to dogs was a low grumble, but he'd pretty much stopped barking at them after day one.

To have a dog outside, eye level with Jace inside, five-to-ten meters away and him not lose his mind was another example of how well he was adapting.

By day three the dogs were no longer following me everywhere I went, which in a small suite wasn't far. It only had a main living area, a bathroom and bedroom.

We continued the longer mid-day walks and on day three went for a short hike on a narrow wooden path through the woods to an open rocky outcrop called Pettinger Point.

I had always avoided closed-in wooded areas because Jace consistently showed high arousal when he was closed in and couldn't see what was coming at him.

Again, he amazed me with his boosted confidence. Yes, he was cautious about each corner we rounded, but his tail was loose and he seemed to enjoy the smells and habitat.

On day four, the day of our 25th wedding anniversary, we decided to make a much longer trek to a local food truck—a Tofino institution. It was just over three kilometres away. We walked the paved path that wound itself alongside the Pacific Rim Highway, and while it's not a terribly busy stretch, and speed limits were low, Jace did seem highly aware. His tail wasn't tucked but he was not confident.

Upon arrival, and realization the lunch line-up was too long to just stand there with the dogs, I found a picnic table and attached both dogs to my hip belt while they went into a down on the table top.

For forty minutes we waited for Barry; Jace was skittish and agitated the entire time.

When he retuned with our burritos, we decided to walk back to the resort and eat them there—it didn't seem fair to make Jace stay in a busy parking lot any longer than necessary. He did extremely well under the circumstances, but I didn't want to push him any more.

Day five was home day.

We had a relaxing sunrise walk as we had each morning, and then breakfast. I decided not to medicate Jace on the return trip considering how well he did on the way, but our packing flurry was definitely affecting both dogs.

Jace was whiny and agitated, Xoco was stoic, but I could sense her discomfort.

The crates were broken down because they had to be packed first, but I laid their cushions on the floor and put them on *place* to try and create some calm. It was a nice try, but it didn't really work.

Jace was more out of sorts in the beginning on that return trip. He finally wore himself out after about two hours of low whining in the back seat and fell asleep. During the wait at Departure Bay Ferry terminal and the ninety-minute crossing back to the mainland he was relaxed.

Getting home was a huge relief for us all, but I think we all missed the surf and laid back family time of Tofino.

It was also a time to reflect on exactly what we had accomplished in the past week and seriously consider when we could do it again.

The author with Jace (foreground) and Xoco in Tofino. Photo: Barry Komar

Month 55:
My Perfectly Imperfect Boy

AS MAY PROGRESSED POST trip and I was putting the final touches on *Jace's Journey*, I was still on the fence about keeping him medicated on Fluoxetine. The date to revisit the discussion with our vet was in June and I still had no true resolution.

I suspected I would go the route of lowering the dosage and seeing how he fared. That seemed like the safest option and the best for Jace in case he really couldn't cope without the support of medication.

The goal was always to help guide him through his constant state of anxiety; a stressful life would most certainly be a shortened one. If the meds helped him live a longer, less stressful life, I would choose that route any day. However, my concern remained; the Fluoxetine could possibly compromise Jace's genetic liver health.

Our sessions with Kelly and her pack of dogs were wrapping up. I continued to be amazed by Jace. His reactions were far less frequent and dramatic, they were short and generally with cause—for example, another dog getting too close or staring.

His ability to recover quickly was notable.

Kelly noticed his body loosening up session after session, and by the last week of May he had actually started sniffing other dogs' butts. It sounded hilarious to be proud of that, but it's how dogs introduce themselves.

Jace had never sniffed another real dog's butt while on-leash. Ever.

He was also stopping to sniff their urine, another hugely positive step forward.

I enjoyed our times with Kelly; her dog sense, her wit, and her eyes on Jace from a trainer's perspective were so beneficial. My intent was to continue these walks in the future, just less frequently. Keeping the momentum going was a priority.

Now that Jace was out more, frequently around stressors and accepting them, he was able to grow, to see that the world wasn't as scary, and other dogs weren't as threatening as he'd believed.

Additionally, with his newfound coping mechanisms he was able to focus more on me. In turn, I was able to use distraction techniques on him to pull his attention away from other dogs when necessary. By being playful, trotting, or quickly turning and luring him with me with treats, or simply saying *no*, I could redirect his focus.

I decided to wrap this book in May, because to me, our family vacation was a massive step forward, and far more successful than I ever dreamed possible.

For the most part I'd taken a terrified dog and got him to a much better place—yes he was still fearful, but also far more equipped to cope with the world around him. He was less concerned with other dogs, or humans in proximity. I felt so much more confident in recalling him when off-leash because he respected me, and the training. As previously stated, his reactivity had diminished incredibly, and his threshold was much higher than it had ever been.

His confidence grew as mine did—the changes in us both were incredible.

Honestly, I didn't yet know what Jace could achieve, but I planned to keep posting about it on *@showmethexolo* and *@jacesjourney_thebook*.

I did not know what our training future would look like, because I was learning as I went—I still am—and remained open to all sorts of direction.

I believed Jace's confidence would continue to grow the longer he was safely exposed to the world. He would always have foundational fear issues, be skittish and mostly untrusting of his environment. But when I read back over these pages of his journey, I saw a dog more resilient than I ever imagined.

What my life, our life, would have looked like if Jace's image had never appeared in my message box almost five years before, I had no idea. I'm sure Barry and I would have continued to raise a new generation of our beloved hairless cats.

I would have missed out on so much though: the challenges, the highs and lows, the sheer encompassing and uncompromising love I had for him, and he for me.

He had made me a better person—more patient, more adaptable and fierce.

He was—and is—my greatest accomplishment; something I achieved not for myself, but for the sake of another being, one who needed me deeply.

He's my perfectly imperfect boy.

PART 12

Be Your Best

HERE IS MY ADVICE.

Find a trainer you trust, one that gets you results. Be open-minded and ask questions; a good trainer will be able to express themselves clearly, and how and if they can help achieve your specific goals. A cheerleader is great, but you're not paying all that money just for positive affirmations.

As they should, all struggling dog owners I've spoken with started solely with positive reinforcement-based training. For many of us that simply wasn't, isn't, enough.

So, if you are not moving forward, find a new trainer—perhaps one with techniques you've never considered. Do your research and ignore anyone who questions your methods. If your dog is safe, loved, and making positive changes, stick with what works. Keep in mind, nothing happens overnight; depending on your dog, it may take months to see notable improvements.

It is so worth investing the time.

Be honest about what your goals are. I know Jace will never be a Xoco and I can live with that, but I couldn't live with myself letting him suffer the way he was before I started his rehabilitation.

If me of today, could go back and talk to me of two, three, or four years ago, what would I stress?

Basic Training

I would have taken a basic puppy-training course—even though Jace was nearly a year old when we got him. Getting Xoco at such a young age, and my desire to set her up for success in life, resulted in me taking a puppy class—even though it was in zoom format, as required during the pandemic. Understanding the very basics of training and engagement, socialization, exposure, and plenty of positive reinforcement also benefitted Jace immensely, even if it was later in his life.

Exposure

As I've noted time and again, exposure is imperative. Jace's lack of it was something I couldn't give him back, but I could have pushed a little more, taken him more places, encouraged him to be curious, and to build his confidence.

Honestly, I still don't know what that would have looked like. He was so fearful from day one I'm not sure what I could have done because he fought me every step of the way. But I should have tried.

Research

While I dabbled in researching dog training, I was only looking at one side of the coin: purely positive. I was also half-assing it. I wish I'd known there were other types of comprehensive training styles sooner. I wish I had taken a deeper dive into dog-training techniques and expanded my level of education. I'm not sure it would have helped in those early days; the lack of balanced and open-minded trainers in my area was an obstacle. I simply wasn't confident enough to tackle training with tools when I first got Jace. I needed so much more guidance.

Walk
Walking your dog tells you so much about them; it also builds engagement if you do it correctly. Just taking them to the off-leash park and hoping they'll wear themselves out, or simply opening the back door and letting them run around the yard will never build your relationship. My bond with Jace improved dramatically once I was able to walk with him; likewise, Xoco. Longer walks are so important. They don't have to be every day, many dogs need down time too; but walk as much as you can; walk together.

Advocate
Give your dog the respect it deserves. That means asking for space when he or she needs it. If your dog doesn't want to meet people or other dogs, don't force it. That doesn't mean complete avoidance, but it does mean being mindful. Each dog is unique and you need to advocate for him or her. That includes telling people to leash their dogs if you feel concerned or threatened. It means telling people they can't touch your dog, or that your dog doesn't do on-leash greetings with other pooches. It means telling people to mind their own business if they question you and your training. If you don't advocate for your dog you will never earn your it's trust.

Ask

Don't be afraid to talk to other people who are struggling. The more I opened up about my own strife, the more people felt secure sharing theirs. I realized there were a lot of people with more experience than me—almost all younger—that had been doing this dog-training thing longer. I watched videos, listened to a wide assortment of folks, and filtered through what made sense. I reached out to them when I had questions, and working through things together we often achieved great things.

Structure

It took me until month 48 to really implement structure in the home. I prioritized fixing issues outside the home, which admittedly I needed to. I feel I would have seen results quicker of I had done both in tandem. Structure and expectation for a dog like Jace was a game-changer. It freed him from having to make choices that were simply making him more anxious. He truly needed to have me, his human, make those decisions for him. Imagine driving a car in a new city, one full of signs, and people, and traffic distracting you while trying to find an address? How much easier would it be if you had someone with you to guide you to your destination, or better yet took the wheel, getting you there safely? It would be a huge relief.

Routine

For a dog like Jace routine is important. Once I'd established that Jace could go for walks and runs with me I started pushing his boundaries slowly, and I would still do exactly that. However, it took me until month 53 to realize his quiet morning walk—a routine—was so important. I stopped trying to push him on those mornings. Rather I kept the same route because he knew it and was comfortable with it. I could still offer him new experiences on other walks, on other days. But he needed to decompress, constant stress was not best for him long term, even if he was handling new stuff with greater confidence. New didn't have to be an everyday occurrence; routine was healthy too.

Fear
There was a lot I was fearful of. I was afraid for Jace, afraid of my lack of trust in him and afraid of people judging me: first for my complete lack of basic dog training skills and control over him; secondly for my use of training tools.

I got over my fear of the latter quite quickly when I realized I had built an online support group, and the results I was seeing in him were unquestionable. The former took a while longer. When I started letting go of fear, my body language changed, as did his responses to the environment, and especially to other dogs.

Confidence
This covers almost everything else I've mentioned above. Confidence breeds success, it protects you from negativity, and it allows you to move forward when you see results. However, it comes with time. How many times did we take one step forward in training, only to get punted two steps back the next day? A lot.

There are still days when my confidence takes a hit, but I'm far better equipped to blow it off. Training a dog like Jace is a marathon, not a sprint; I now have the understanding and determination to succeed.

You

You do you. Don't fall into the trap of measuring your successes, or rehabilitation speed to anyone else's. Social media can drag you down when you see dogs achieving great things. Competition style heeling looks amazing, but if you don't need it, don't sweat it. Focus on your dog and what it needs to be fulfilled; focus on your needs and what those look like to you. Once you've built a solid foundation of basic skills, communication, and trust, then the next steps are totally up to you.

Forgive

I had a lot of guilt when it came to Jace, but nothing could change the past so I had to let go. Writing this book helped me understand where I went wrong, but it also showed me how far we've come. Knowing my written experience might help someone else also goes a long way toward forgiveness. I know Jace doesn't blame me.

As the quote by *Maya Angelou* at the start of this book says, "Do the best you can until you know better. Then when you know better, do better."

I guarantee, just like me, you're doing your best right now.